To Rod + Ducke Ph

May God Bless
Your Ministry!

Understanding the Generations

Understanding the Generations

James L. Knapp, Ph.D.

Aventine Press

Published by Aventine Press
1023 4th Ave #204
San Diego CA, 92101
www.aventinepress.com

ISBN: 1-59330-329-7

To my parents, Lyle and Donna Knapp

Forward

Many individuals have contributed to the development of this book. First, and foremost, are the hundreds of church leaders and members who completed a survey or agreed to be interviewed. I am deeply appreciative of their generosity and recognize that without their input, this book would not have been possible.

Second, Southeastern Oklahoma State University has played a significant role by providing financial support through a Faculty Research Grant. In addition, Margo Wright served as a valuable research assistant during the data collection phase.

Third, I am deeply indebted to several individuals who have encouraged me during the process of writing the manuscript. A heartfelt "thank you" is extended to Joe Ed Furr, Charlie Pruett, and Jim Hughes.

Finally, my family continues to provide immeasurable support and encouragement to me. Tracy, Ashley, and Andrew, thank you for your patience.

Table of Contents

Chapter 1 – The Power of a Generation.................................1

Chapter 2 – A Century of Change.......................................11

Chapter 3 – Senior Adults (1926 or earlier)..........................23

Chapter 4 – Builders (1927-1945)......................................31

Chapter 5 – Boomers (1946-1964)......................................41

Chapter 6 – GenXers (1965-1983)......................................53

Chapter 7 – Millennials (1984-2002)..................................63

Chapter 8 – A Biblical Perspective on Generations........73

Chapter 9 – A Congregational Response.......................85

Epilogue...99

Appendix A: Resources...103

Appendix B: Methodology..105

Chapter Notes..109

Chapter 1
The Power of a Generation

In March of 1969, Margaret Mead accepted an invitation to speak at the American Museum of Natural History. During her lecture, the renowned anthropologist described three types of cultures and how the interaction of generations varied in each. According to Mead, a post-figurative culture was characterized by children learning the skills necessary for survival from their parents, grandparents, and other adults. Because things changed very slowly, the future for the youngest generation was nearly identical to that experienced by the oldest generation. In a co-figurative culture, children and adults relied heavily on their peers for knowledge and skills. While the oldest generation was still dominate, a shift in power and influence was occurring as younger generations were shaped by their contemporaries more than their elders. In a pre-figurative culture, younger generations continued to be influenced by older generations but the inverse was true, as well. Changing cultural patterns and a shift in the knowledge base forced members of the older generations to rely on those in the younger generations for guidance in the new social order. Based on her examination of American society, Mead concluded that the United States had become a pre-figurative culture.[1]

It was also in this lecture that Mead made two bold yet profound statements.[2] In the first, she declared that "... the continuity of all cultures depends on the living presence of at least three generations." Her second statement, that "... all of us who were born and reared before the 1940s are immigrants" may have been shocking at the time but more than thirty years later it is amazingly astute. Mead was describing the condition of the late 20th and early 21st centuries in which the various generations desperately need each other but often struggle to find common ground.

It is this condition of "confused interdependence" that will be addressed in the pages that follow. After surveying the cultural forces that shaped American life in the 20th century (Chapter 2), one chapter will be dedicated to each of the five living generations (Chapters 3-7). Each chapter will review the significant events that occurred during that era and discuss the perspective that is commonly found among members of the generation. In the final two chapters, an application of the information will be made to Protestant churches. Chapter 8 will provide a Biblical perspective on generations and Chapter 9 will focus on how congregations can effectively blend the generations. Before proceeding, however, it is necessary to develop a working knowledge of generations and to understand why a generational perspective is such a powerful force.

What is a Generation?

A generation usually covers a span of 15 to 20 years. Including the word "usually" is important because it is possible for a generation to extend beyond 20 years if certain conditions are present. When war or extreme famine occurs, individuals may postpone getting married and starting a family until the crisis has been resolved. Shifts in the economy can also affect the beginning of a new generation. For instance, it can be argued that the increase in the number of women receiving college degrees and subsequently entering the paid labor force has had the unintended consequence of extending the upper limit of the generational range. In most cases, however, conditions such as these have a greater impact on the number of babies born within the time frame as opposed to altering its length. Thus, the 15 to 20 year range is accurate because it is during this interval that the oldest members of the preceding generation develop the ability to bear children and begin a new generation.

While the element of time is an important part of defining a generation, it pales in comparison to a second factor. A fundamental characteristic of a generation is that the members move through the life cycle together and experience significant historical events at approximately the same age. As a result, they develop a lens through which to see the world and a set of beliefs that are used to interpret the events that occur around them. Research has indicated that events which transpire during one's formative years are extremely important in shaping their generational lens and continue to be used throughout the remainder of their life.[3] As an example, the hardships that characterized the Great Depression had a lasting impact on persons who lived through it. For those who were teenagers or in their early adult years, the events of that period in history were deeply seared into their memory. More than seventy years later, many who experienced the Great Depression continue to be frugal and more inclined to save their money than spend it.

Does a Gap Exist?

As Margaret Mead noted about post-figurative cultures, things change very slowly because the younger generations rely on the older generations to teach them how to survive. This form of intergenerational transfer was very common in the United States when the economy was based primarily on agriculture. Farming methods had been refined to the point that what was done in the past continued to be done in the present because they had proven to be effective. It was generally assumed that the existing methods would be used in the future so the need to explore new possibilities rarely materialized. As a result, there was great continuity across the generations and whatever gap may have existed was very small. When the movement from an agricultural society to an industrial (and later a postindustrial) society began, the continuity between the generations changed dramatically. As young people left the farm, the position of power and influence that had been held by the oldest generation began to decline. The need to own land was no longer important to a generation that was sufficiently employed in urban settings. When the next generation filled college classrooms and prepared for white-collar jobs, this pattern repeated itself and the distance between the generations began to increase.

The shift in the economic base had a noticeable impact on how the generations interacted with one another not only because of the type of work that was being done but also due to the rapid technological and cultural change that accompanied it. New value systems, changing patterns of family life, and a redefinition of religious expectations were but a few of the changes that appeared. As these occurred, the ancient Chinese proverb that "… men resemble the times more than their fathers" became very apparent. Younger generations began to blend what they had inherited from previous generations with those things that were being experienced in their rapidly changing social world. The result was a new set of values and beliefs that seemed appropriate to them but puzzled members of their parent's and grandparent's generations.

This process reached a critical stage during the 1960s and gave birth to the expression "generation gap". Since then, "generation gap" has been overused but when applied correctly it accurately describes the tension which can exist between members of different generations. Since each generation views the world through a lens that was shaped during its formative years and since the pace of social and technological change was so rapid during the 20th century, it is little wonder that tensions have existed between the generations. The analogy of a lens has also given rise to the expression "generational myopia" which describes the inability of one generation to see the world from any perspective other than its own.[4] In order to understand how the members of a different generation think and why they act in the manner they do, it is necessary to see the world through their lens. Even if one does not agree with that perspective, it sheds new light on the values, beliefs, and behaviors of that generation.

Where generational myopia is present, a generation gap is sure to follow. An inability, or an unwillingness, to see the world through a different lens will inevitably drive a wedge between the generations. The result will be a fragmented society, community, church, or family. An effective way to counter the presence of a generation gap is to develop a working knowledge of the perspectives held by other generations. With that in mind, the primary purpose of this book is to increase awareness of other generations and their perspectives in order to create an environment that encourages positive intergenerational relationships.

5 Living Generations

At the beginning of the 21st century, there are five living generations in the United States.[5] Though a detailed examination of each generation will be provided in subsequent chapters, a brief introduction will be provided here.

Senior Adults

Senior Adults are the oldest living generation in the United States. Born before 1927, Senior Adults are now in their eighth decade of life or beyond and represent 5% of the American population. While this figure seems insignificant, against the backdrop of human history it is phenomenal. Due to the harsh conditions that existed in pre-industrial societies, most individuals struggled to reach their fourth or fifth decade of life. Even when Senior Adults were born, life expectancy in the United States was less than fifty years and very few individuals lived beyond their seventh decade. During the 20th century, however, improvements in medical care, food preservation, and sanitation made it possible for a greater number of Americans to experience this stage of life.

Of the five living generations, Senior Adults have experienced the greatest transformation of their world. When they were children, the automobile was still in its infancy, commercial air travel did not exist and the majority of Americans made their living on small farms by relying heavily on manual labor. In terms of education, anything beyond the 3 R's was considered a luxury and only the most fortunate even dreamed of attending college. Despite being raised in these circumstances, Senior Adults have displayed an amazing level of resiliency as they have adapted to the challenges and opportunities of the 20th and early 21st centuries. Due to their longevity, Senior Adults are a living link to the past for the general population, as well as communities of faith.

Builders

Born between 1927 and 1945, Builders overcame a significant number of obstacles during their formative years since the bulk of this generation arrived between the start of the Great Depression and the conclusion of World War II. Nevertheless, they emerged victorious from the war and earned their name by creating the economic abundance that Americans enjoyed for years to come. With the help of the GI Bill, Builders attended college or trade school in mass, bought homes in communities like Levittown, and worked diligently to provide a better existence for their children than they had experienced. Arguably, however, the Builder's most significant contribution to American society was the baby boom they created in the post war years. With stable, well-paying jobs readily available, Builders were able to support a massive number of children. Once they arrived, Builders committed themselves to raising their offspring in wholesome environments that placed a premium on family values and belief in God.

Builders now range in age from the early 60s to the late 70s and represent 14% of the American population.

While many have entered the retirement years, some are still actively involved in the labor force and a significant number occupy leadership positions in their communities and churches.

Boomers

The Baby Boomers are America's largest and most powerful generation. Born between 1946 and 1964, 27% of Americans are Boomers. Due to their enormous size, Boomers have had an extraordinary influence on American society. In the late 1940s and especially during the 1950s, maternity wards were filled to capacity and community planners scrambled to build enough homes, schools, and parks to accommodate the Boomers. College and university enrollments soared during the 1960s and 1970s as Boomers equipped themselves to enter the increasingly complex labor force. Upon arrival, they altered the rules of engagement as company loyalty took a backseat to self-actualization and the pursuit of personal financial gain particularly during the "yuppie" years.

Boomers are now in their fourth or fifth decade of life and family responsibilities occupy much of their time. In recent years, the expression "sandwich generation" has been used to describe the situation of many Boomers as they try to raise their children while simultaneously care for their aging parents. At the same time, Boomers have risen to leadership positions in their careers, communities, and churches. Their willingness to think and act in unconventional ways is now exerting a tremendous influence in those settings and will continue to do so for many years to come.

Generation X

Born between 1965 and 1983, 27% of Americans are GenXers. Though they are a large and unique group, GenXers had the misfortune of being born immediately after the Baby Boomers. Growing up in the shadow of such a transforming generation has been difficult for GenXers. Their beliefs, values, and behaviors have been heavily criticized and they have often been referred to as apathetic, cynical, and malcontents.[6] Even the name Generation "X", which many of them despise, sends the message that they lack a clear identity or purpose in life.

The maturation of Generation X coincided with two significant forces. The first was the technological explosion of the late 20th century. GenXers were raised with computers, cell phones, and hand-held video games. As a result, they are a technologically-savvy group that relies heavily on visual presentations rather than the printed or spoken word. The second force that strongly influenced Generation X was the emergence of postmodernism into the mainstream of society. While postmodernism encompasses a wide range of beliefs and ideas, one of its primary tenants is that absolute truth does not exist. This presents a formidable challenge to any religion or belief system that claims to offer the one and only truth.

Millennials

The youngest of the five living generations is the Millennials. Since the majority of Millennials are still in their pre-teen years, it is difficult to make definitive statements about them. Nevertheless, the information that is beginning to trickle in suggests a transition is underway. In contrast to the skepticism of Generation

X, Millennials seem to be exhibiting a more optimistic
view of life. To some degree, the characteristics of the
Builders are reappearing as Millennials display a high level
of maturity even at this early stage of their development.
One thing that can be confirmed about Millennials is their
size. Born between 1984 and 2002, Millennials represent
27% of the population and are on their way to becoming
a generation larger than the Baby Boomers.

Summary

The presence of five living generations is unique
to the 20th and 21st centuries but the dynamic of
intergenerational relationships is not. From the earliest
days of human history, members of multiple generations
have lived and worked together with varying levels of
success. In the past one hundred years, the pace of social
and economic change quickened dramatically which
presented a formidable challenge to the bonds that held
the generations together. In Chapter 2, we will survey
the cultural landscape of 20th century America in order
to understand the forces that impacted generational
relationships.

Chapter 2
A Century of Change

The 20th century in America was a paradox. It was a collection of trends and events that seemed to be at odds with each other. For instance, the greatest economic decline in the history of our nation (the Great Depression) occurred in the same century that saw middle-class households more than triple their annual income (as measured in constant dollars)[1]. Using the power of scientific discovery, medical researchers waged war with early childhood diseases and effectively eliminated them from our consideration. Along the way, however, new diseases like AIDS and Alzheimer's Disease were uncovered. The same technology that was used to end the Second World War quickly became the source of the Cold War. In other words, the gains of the 20th century were accompanied by a new set of challenges.

It is not our purpose in this chapter to evaluate the merits of the 20th century and whether or not our society was in better condition in 1999 than 1900. It is important to recognize, however, that the 20th century in America was characterized by enormous change. A century that began with horse travel and telegraphs ended with space shuttles and cell phones. Along the way, the people who lived in this country were influenced by the changes. Our

views of family, work, education, and religion, to name
just a few, were crafted during the century. Thus, if we
intend to understand how the generational perspectives
emerged, we must first take a sociological glimpse at what
occurred in the United States during the 20th century.

Leaving the Farm

During the early years of the 20th century, more
than five million American families made their living
on a farm.[2] Many of these farms were small operations
that provided a means of support for a nuclear family
and, at times, an extended family. While agricultural
production continued to be a significant contributor
to the American economy well into the century, life on
the farm underwent monumental changes. Productivity
began to increase as tractors replaced horses and mules,
pesticides and fertilizers gave farmers more control over
their crop production, and the Dust Bowl of the 1930s
forced many small farmers to abandon their land and
find another form of work. What emerged were fewer
farmers with extremely large farms. Between 1950 and
1998, the size of the average farm doubled despite the fact
that the number of Americans employed in agriculture
decreased by 53%.[3]

For landowners who had assumed that farming
would remain a stable occupation for themselves and
their children, the changing status of agriculture had a
ripple effect. In addition to the changing technological
requirements, farmers increasingly found that many
of their adult children were not interested in making
their living in agriculture. Following World War I, a
massive migration from rural to urban areas began to
occur. The lure of manufacturing jobs, with regular

paychecks and steady hours, enticed many young people to abandon farm life and move to cities where this type of employment existed. In the first two decades of the century, the percentage of Americans living in rural areas dropped from 60% to 50%. This pattern became more pronounced as the century progressed with only one in four Americans living in a rural area in 1999.[4]

A New Idea of Family

Following a substantial decline during the Great Depression, the fertility rate soared during the 1950s and returned to the level that existed at the beginning of the 20th century. After the 1950s, however, the fertility rate steadily declined reaching a record low of 1.8 children per woman in 1976. By the end of the century, the fertility rate had inched its way back to 2.07 children per woman but was still far below the numbers that were typical during the first half of the century.[5]

The reduced size of the American family can be linked to at least three factors. First, the movement away from an agricultural economy meant that fewer children were needed to work on the farm. In the past it was necessary to have an abundance of "free" labor in order for the family farm to remain viable. To a large degree the family was viewed as an economic unit and every member was expected to contribute to the good of the unit by performing age-appropriate chores. The shift to an industrial and, later, a postindustrial society meant that the decision to have children could be based on factors other than maintaining the family farm.

Second, the sexual revolution of the 20th century dramatically changed many American's attitude toward sex. Though the "Roaring Twenties" were characterized by considerable sexual freedom, it was not until the 1960s that the sexual revolution became widespread. A major contributor to the increased freedom was the arrival of "The Pill" in 1960.[6] With its introduction, a couple could enjoy the sexual experience more spontaneously than before but still be protected against an unwanted pregnancy. This meant that men and women had greater control over the number of children they had without having to abstain from intercourse.

The third contributing factor to smaller families was the monumental increase in the number of women in the labor force. Following World War II, "Rosie the Riveter" resumed her pre-war role in the home and was replaced in the factories by the returning GIs. By the 1960s, however, married women were entering the labor force at an unprecedented rate. Fueled in part by Betty Friedan's book, *The Feminine Mystique*, many females began to question the idea that a woman's place was in the home and became more assertive in their desire to attend college and enter professions that had once been reserved for men. As a result, the number of married women in the labor force grew from 25% to 61% between 1960 and 1998. More importantly, the number of married women with children under the age of 6 who were participating in the labor force increased from 12% in 1950 to 64% in 1998.[7]

Not only has the size of the American family changed but the definition of what constitutes a family has been altered, as well. At the beginning of the century, 80% of all households were headed by a married couple. By 1998, the figure had dropped to 53%.[8] Some of the decline was due to a larger number of elderly individuals living alone following the death of a spouse. The growth in the number of cohabiting couples from 523,000 in 1970 to 4.2 million in 1998 also contributed to the increase.[9] Most importantly, however, has been the significant increase in the number of single-parent families since 1960. Whether due to divorce, desertion, death of a spouse, or an out-of-wedlock birth, at the end of the century roughly one third of all children in America did not live with two parents.[10]

Higher Education

Prior to entering World War II, less than 25% of Americans had graduated from high school. In the years that followed the war, the number increased sharply so that by 1998 more than 80% of Americans had a high school diploma.[11] College graduation rates, though not as pronounced, also increased from 3% to 24% in the latter half of the century.[12]

Post World War II America brought the advent of federal programs to aid students who desired a higher education. Previously, a student and his or her family were solely responsible for paying the expenses related to receiving a college education unless a scholarship could be obtained. During the 1950s and 1960s, numerous grant and loan programs, backed by the federal government, were introduced. The result was a steady stream of teenagers pursuing college degrees. Many veterans also appeared on college campuses as the GI Bill allowed them to continue their formal education by receiving technical training or pursuing a college education. By the late 1960s and early 1970s, colleges and universities experienced unprecedented growth due to the baby boom generation reaching their late teens and early twenties.

College enrollment also meant that young men could be deferred from military service in Vietnam.

While some retrenchment has occurred since the early 1970s, colleges and universities continue to play a vital role in American society. In their role as institutions of higher learning, colleges and universities are designed not only to provide white-collar vocational training but to stretch the minds of students by exposing them to art, culture, literature, and philosophy outside of their own experience. The intended result is to produce well-rounded individuals who are capable of handling new ideas and effectively communicating them. Individuals who possess these skills are essential in the global, information age of the 21st century. However, they can pose a considerable challenge in settings that are guided by tradition and for institutions that place a high premium on maintaining the status quo.

Technology

Of all the changes that occurred in the United States during the 20th century, the growing presence of technology may have been the most significant. Whether it was household conveniences, automobiles, or computers, the ever-increasing reliance of Americans on technological advances was stunning. In less than 100 years, a society built on manual labor and horsepower had become dependent on microchips and satellites.

The mechanization of the American home provides an excellent illustration of the growth of technology. When the 20th century began, most homes were not equipped with the conveniences that are now considered to be standard features. A key ingredient in the rapid advancement of technology was gaining access to electricity. Between 1900 and 1950, the number of homes receiving electrical service increased from 2% to 94%.[13] When coupled with other technological developments, electricity opened the door to a variety of domestic items. For instance, refrigeration in private homes was unheard of in 1900 but by mid-century 80% of Americans owned a refrigerator.[14] Air conditioners, which were rarely seen in the middle of the century, were cooling 78% of American homes by 1997.[15] The clearest example of technology in American homes, however, was the presence of television. In 1946, there were only 8,000 television sets in the entire country. Less than a decade later the number had skyrocketed to 26 million. By the end of the century, 98% of American households had at least one television set which was being used an average of seven hours per day.[16]

In the closing decades of the 20th century, the World Wide Web brought global destinations into the homes and offices of a growing number of Americans. During the 1990s, personal computer ownership and access to the World Wide Web grew so rapidly that by the end of the 20th century 42% of American households were equipped with a personal computer and nearly one in three were linked to the World Wide Web.[17]

Rethinking Religion

During the first half of the 20th century, organized religion in America maintained the high degree of visibility it had enjoyed for many decades. Though the economic difficulties of the Great Depression had limited the ability of churches to engage in building projects or extensive missionary work, participation in organized religion remained at the core of the American experience.[18]

As the Second World War ended and civilian life resumed, it seemed hard to imagine that the presence of Christianity in America could increase but it did. The results of numerous public opinion polls reported that Americans were becoming even more religious. The National Opinion Research Center reported in 1946 that two out of every three Americans attended religious services at least once a month and 42% attended every week.[19]

Not surprisingly, membership in religious organizations also soared during the 1940s and 1950s. The largest Protestant denomination, the United Methodist Church, reported a membership in excess of eight million people. The rapidly expanding Southern Baptist Church was a close second with more than six million members and the Presbyterian Church (at that time divided into northern and southern branches) was third with nearly 3 million members. Even a comparatively small religious group like the Church of Christ was experiencing unprecedented growth with a membership of approximately 800,000 people.[20] The influence of Christianity in America was so widespread that the federal government added the words "one nation under God" to the pledge of allegiance and "in God we trust" to U.S. currency in 1954.[21]

Christianity was such a prominent part of life in the United States that it was difficult to see the decline that was looming on the horizon. Despite the intense exposure to organized religion they had received earlier in life, by the 1960s a large number of young adults set aside their religious heritage and began a journey of spiritual exploration. For some the journey was short-lived and involved nothing more than "sowing their wild oats". For a significant group of others, however, their departure marked the end of the rapid expansion of mainline Protestant churches and began a steady movement away from organized religion. Disenchanted with their religious roots and convinced that mainline churches were unable or unwilling to respond to the issues they were wrestling with, young people in the 1960s and 1970s turned to other sources for wisdom and meaning including Buddhism, Taoism, self-help philosophies, and hybrid forms of Christianity.

Clearly, the religious landscape was altered during the 20th century. The focus on organized religion gave way to a more individualized quest for meaning and relationship with God. The shift prompted many to conclude that Americans were less religious at the end of the 20th century than they were previously. This conclusion, however, failed to consider that many Americans remained very interested in religion and spiritual growth albeit in non-traditional ways.[22]

PostModernism

Finally, a shift from a modern to a postmodern view of the world began to occur during the first half of the 20th century. In order to understand the significance of this change, a brief review of western civilization is necessary.

Historians refer to the events that occurred in Western Europe during the 16th century as the Renaissance. Following the Dark Ages, when intellectual development had been very limited, the Renaissance was characterized by a renewed interest in the classical spirit of learning that had existed during the Greek and Roman civilizations. Renaissance thinkers placed human beings at the heart of the universe, began to question the unchecked authority that churches and monarchies held, and became advocates for the use of the scientific method in order to understand the workings of the universe.[23] They believed that by using the power of scientific discovery, the irrational aspects of society could be exposed and replaced with a better social order. The new society would be devoid of superstition and irrationality and based instead on rational thought informed by the scientific method.[24]

Though the ultimate goal of Renaissance thinkers (and those that followed during the Enlightenment of the 17th and 18th centuries) was never reached, the impact of the progress they did make can be clearly seen in the United States. Through the middle part of the 20th century, American society was guided by the belief that objective knowledge was obtainable and that it could be used to rationally manage life.[25] Scientific advancements, it was believed, could lead to better technologies which would then lead to a better quality of life for all Americans.

While modernism flourished in the first half of the 20th century, postmodernism was very quietly being introduced. The term postmodernism was first used in the 1930s to refer to an emerging trend in art and to describe a reaction to modernism. In its early days, postmodernism was an obscure philosophy championed by a very small group of proponents. Gradually, however, postmodernism began to gain support so that by the 1960s, a sizeable number of artists, architects, and intellectuals were openly discussing it in their writing and teaching.[26]

At its most basic level, postmodernism refers to a way of thinking and a means of expressing discontent with the ideals, values, and principles that characterize modernism.[27] In the modern mindset, knowledge is considered to be good, attainable, and objective. The continuing quest for knowledge that is characteristic of the modernist is fueled by an optimistic view that additional knowledge will inevitably lead to progress which in turn will lead to a better social order. In the postmodern mindset, the optimistic line of reasoning that drives modernism is rejected and replaced with a pessimistic view of the future and a full-scale rejection of the notion of absolute truth.[28] Rather than trying to discover a single, absolute, objective truth through reason and scientific endeavors (referred to as a meta-narrative or the grand theme that guides the entire universe), postmodernists emphasize that each person must come to understand how truth is created in the context of the local communities in which he or she participates. Thus, truth is relative to postmodernists. In addition, postmodernists emphasize that there are other ways to attain knowledge beyond the rational processes endorsed by the scientific method. Intuition and emotion are encouraged in the postmodern mindset and considered to be valid avenues through which knowledge can be attained.[29]

Summary

Life in the United States was noticeably different at the end of the 20th century compared to the beginning. Changes in economic arrangements, family composition, higher education, and technology occurred throughout the century and impacted the daily activities of Americans. Each of the five living generations joined this journey at different points which led to the development of unique perspectives as they blended inherited information with personal experiences. Senior Adults were the first to participate in this process and will be the focus of Chapter 3.

Chapter 3
Senior Adults
(1926 or earlier)

For years, Henry Ford had dreamed of building a car for the masses and in October of 1908, he did. Prior to the Model T, only 2,500 cars were being produced annually in the United States but the arrival of the "Tin Lizzie" significantly altered the floundering automobile industry and put car ownership in reach of millions of Americans. At first, his board of directors did not like the idea but Ford insisted that consumers would buy an automobile if it was reasonably priced and readily available. His intuition was correct as 10,000 Model T's were sold during the first year of production at a cost of $825 per car. Over the next few years, the price dropped so that by 1912, a Model T could be purchased for less than $575.[1]

When production ceased in 1927, more than 15 million Model T's had been sold and the American landscape had changed. No longer dependent on trains or horse and buggies as their sole means of transportation, Americans became more mobile. Even though road construction lagged behind, the opportunity to travel at one's own pace and in the relative comfort of an automobile was highly appealing and millions of Americans capitalized on it. As the number of travelers increased, so did the breadth of services designed for them. Restaurants, motels, and roadside attractions gradually began to appear along major thoroughfares as automobile travel developed into an experience for the masses.

While the Model T clearly impacted the mobility of Americans, it also affected the employment experience. Soon after its introduction, Ford began to assemble the Model T in a new facility that standardized the process and increased the number of units that could be produced. As a result, Model T's were rolling off the assembly line at lightening speeds that left competitors in awe. Proponents of scientific management applauded the efficiency of Ford's production process but opponents argued that the assembly line was dehumanizing to the workers as they engaged in mindless, repetitive work day after day. Initially, the concerns were ignored since a multitude of poorly educated immigrants was available to fill the positions. In time, however, employees began to leave due to poor working conditions combined with low pay. Since he couldn't change the process of production, Ford decided to alter the pay scale. In January of 1914, he established the first minimum wage of $5 for an eight hour day and the labor shortage was corrected.

Suffrage & Spirits

While Henry Ford was changing the way Americans worked and traveled, a group of activists were trying to expand the rights of women in the United States. Of principle concern to them was the right to vote, an issue that had emerged as early as 1848. Under the leadership of individuals like Susan B. Anthony, activists worked tirelessly during the late 19th century to increase awareness of the rights that were being denied to women. Despite their hard work, they were faced with strong opposition and only modest success was experienced. While the Wyoming and Utah territories extended suffrage to women in 1869 and 1870, respectively, it wasn't until the first two decades of the 20th century that the issue of a woman's right to vote gained national prominence.[2] As a growing number of states passed suffrage referendums, the pressure for women to be granted the opportunity to participate in national elections continued to mount. Even President Woodrow Wilson became a part of the debate as he addressed the National American Woman Suffrage Movement. By 1919, it became apparent that Americans were ready to include women in the electoral process at all levels. With a joint resolution from Congress, the Nineteenth Amendment to the Constitution was sent to the states for ratification and on August 26, 1920, women received the right to vote in national elections.

At approximately the same time, another high profile social issue was being debated. Following the Civil War, the United States had experienced significant economic growth but many citizens felt that the morality of the nation had declined. In response, the Progressive movement gained momentum during the early years of the 20th century and a variety of social reforms were proposed. Among them was an effort to ban the production and distribution of alcohol. While opposition to the ban could be found, support for prohibition was widespread especially among groups like the Allied Citizens of America and the Woman's Christian Temperance Union.[3]

The evils of alcohol, in any form or quantity, became the focus of magazine articles, sermons, and even

political speeches. As a result, Congress adopted the 18th
Amendment in December of 1917 and submitted it to the
citizens. Since numerous states and counties already had
"dry laws" in place, the amendment was easily ratified and
on January 17, 1920 constitutional prohibition went into
effect. Throughout the 1920s and into the early 1930s,
it was illegal to manufacture, distribute, or sell alcohol
though breweries were still permitted to produce a low-
alcohol drink known as "near-beer".[4]

A Snapshot of America: 1920

Compared to the volumes of information that are
generated by the Census Bureau today, the 1920 census
seems to lack the depth needed to adequately understand
life in the United States during that era. A closer
examination, however, reveals that it is possible to catch
a glimpse of the American experience when members
of the Senior Adult generation were in their formative
years.

In 1920, there were 106 million Americans (compared
to 290 million in 2004) and nearly half of them lived
in a rural area. Formal education was emphasized for
children between the ages of seven and thirteen as 91%
attended school but once they had attained a basic level
of education, many either did not or could not continue
in school. Less than half of sixteen and seventeen year
olds continued their education opting instead to work
on the farm or join the paid labor force. In many ways,
this was a wise decision since more than half of the
jobs available in the United States were in agriculture or
manufacturing. Employment in professional fields like
law, engineering, and medicine were not abundant and
required extensive formal education which was beyond

the means of most Americans. A typical family had 4.3 persons in it and was likely to have begun during the husband and wife's teenage years. More than 60% of persons over the age of fifteen were married and for the most part, the division of labor was clearly defined. Men were seen as being the primary breadwinner for the family while women were expected to support their husband's efforts. Though women possessed valuable skills, they were usually applied in the home as less than one in four females was gainfully employed.[5]

Characteristics of the Generation

It was in this environment that Senior Adults were born and raised. While subsequent generations have experienced portions of the social, economic, and technological transformation that occurred during the 20th century, in a sense, Senior Adults have seen it all. During their lifetime, automobiles have gone from being a novelty to an essential part of everyday life and women, who were not permitted to vote in most state or any national elections at the beginning of the 20th century, now serve as governors, representatives, and senators.

As these and many other changes have come about, Senior Adults have adapted. Though they often speak fondly of days gone by and frequently compare the current state of affairs to the era in which they were raised, Senior Adults have consistently displayed a high level of resiliency. Now, as they range in age from 80 to 100 and beyond, many Senior Adults are faced with yet another challenge as they respond to a loss of health, independence, status, and loved ones.

As they enter the later years and deal with the issues that often accompany this stage of life, Senior Adults should not be pushed to the margins because they represent a vital link to the past. Having experienced two world wars, an extreme economic depression, numerous social upheavals, and eighteen presidential administrations, Senior Adults can augment textbooks by sharing their personal accounts of those events. The wealth of knowledge and experience that exists in this segment of the population should be respected and treated as the treasure that it is. This is applicable in society at large, as well as the local church. Though they are often accused of standing in the way of progress and zealously defending selected forms of worship and ministry, Senior Adults can bring a calming stability to a church that is searching for direction.

Although they presently represent 5% of the American population, the Senior Adult generation is gradually fading from view. While some are able to maintain a high level of involvement in church and civic activities, a growing number are experiencing chronic health problems which limit their mobility. Churches should remain cognizant of their Senior Adult members and be especially attentive to those who need assistance even though they may not be able to participate in the worship assemblies.

Senior Adults: An Illustration

Betty Miller has lived in the same house her entire life. Born on November 12, 1922 in the small community of Vienna, West Virginia, Betty was the youngest child of Curt and Rosa Miller. During her childhood, she spent countless hours playing with her older sister, attending church, and relishing the Sunday afternoon gatherings at the Miller home following the morning worship service.

After completing her high school education, Betty attended Freed-Hardeman College in Tennessee where she earned an associate's degree in education. She returned to Vienna in 1943 and taught at a one-room school before moving to a larger elementary school in 1944. While teaching full-time, Betty continued her own education and in 1947 she completed a bachelor's degree from Marshall University in Huntington, West Virginia after which she began graduate study at Peabody Teacher's College (now a part of Vanderbilt University) in Nashville, Tennessee. Since she was only able to attend classes during the summer, her progress was slow but Betty's persistence paid off in 1952 when she was awarded a master's degree in elementary education. After she retired from the public school system, Betty was asked to teach at Ohio Valley College (OVC). A small, church-affiliated school located a few minutes from her home, OVC provided a second career for Betty and allowed her to work with adult students which she thoroughly enjoyed.

Throughout her years as an educator, Betty continued to live with her parents and older sister, June. As June's health began to decline due to cerebral palsy and as her parents experienced difficulties associated with their advanced age, Betty willingly accepted the role of caregiver. She dedicated her time and energy to providing the highest quality of care she could until each member of her immediate family passed away.

For more than 70 years, Betty has been a member of the 36th Street Church of Christ (formerly the Pleasant Avenue Church of Christ) in Vienna. During those years, she saw her father serve as an elder and teacher while her mother taught in her home, practiced hospitality, and baked the communion bread that was used each Sunday. Betty has followed in her parent's footsteps by being a Bible class teacher since the 1950s, speaking at lectureships and workshops for women, visiting the sick, and serving in an unheralded way to those who need encouragement or assistance.

In some ways, Betty Miller is an exception to the norm. Her high level of formal education was unusual for her generation and was particularly unique for females. In other ways, she is the embodiment of the Senior Adult generation. Betty's commitment to family and lifelong involvement with one church, even during periods of transition, illustrates the stability that has characterized the Senior Adult generation.

Summary

The Senior Adult generation is an excellent illustration of Margaret Mead's statement that those "who were born and reared before the 1940s are immigrants." Due to their longevity, Senior Adults have seen monumental social and economic shifts but have consistently found a way to adapt. In Chapter 4, another group that has seen sweeping change in their world will be introduced as we examine the Builder generation.

Chapter 4
Builders
(1927-1945)

Following World War I, an economic recession occurred in many countries. However, life in the United States during the "Roaring Twenties" was characterized by prosperity and extravagance until October of 1929. While signs of the impending crash of the stock market appeared earlier, most business leaders and high-ranking government officials dismissed the indicators as an aberration in an otherwise stable economy. The optimistic rhetoric began to fade when the reality of over speculation and questionable investing strategies became apparent. On October 29, stocks plummeted in value and individuals whose wealth resided in the stock market saw their fortune disappear.

For those who made their living in agriculture, the impact of the Depression was not immediately felt. Most farmers worked comparatively small tracts of land and their involvement with financial institutions was limited to the bank that held a lien against their property. During the 1930s, however, adverse climatic conditions and a depressed economy staggered farmers particularly those who lived in the Midwest. A large percentage of farmland became unusable due to a lack of rain and gusting winds that blew away the top soil. In addition, the market value of the crops that were produced declined in value.[1]

The impact of the Depression and Dust Bowl on America was significant. A population shift ensued as many farm families headed west in search of a better life with California being the destination of choice. Upon arrival, some families became migrant farm workers but a far greater number located in or around urban areas like Los Angeles.[2] The Depression and Dust Bowl also changed the way American's viewed the federal government which gave birth to the New Deal of Franklin Delano Roosevelt (FDR).

The New Deal

During his acceptance speech at the Democratic National Convention in 1932, presidential hopeful FDR declared a "new deal for the American people." In the first one hundred days of his presidency, he followed through in earnest on his promise as a number of new programs were initiated including the Federal Deposit Insurance Corporation (FDIC), Securities and Exchange Commission, and the National Industrial Recovery Act which guaranteed workers the right to collective bargaining. The array of government programs also included the Civilian Conservation Corp that was designed for the needy who could not find work. Young men between the ages of 18 and 25 who were single and in good physical condition enlisted for an initial term of six months that could be renewed for a maximum of two years. They lived in military-style camps and built roads, recreation areas, and lodges at state parks. In addition to receiving clothes, a bed to sleep in, and three hot meals per day, the men were paid $30 a month of which they sent $22 to $25 home to help support their family.[3]

A second wave of programs was launched in 1935 including the Works Progress Administration, which created hundred of jobs albeit at an extremely low level of pay, and the Social Security Administration. In its original form, Social Security provided immediate relief to older Americans who were poor as well as a second component that established a retirement savings plan that would be managed by the federal government. In subsequent years, Social Security was modified and expanded but its initial purpose was to create a financial security net for the elderly.

While the New Deal did not end the Depression, it did alter the American experience. Prior to FDR's administration, the federal government was relatively small and the only direct contact most citizens had with it was their interaction with the postal service. During the 1930s, the size of the federal government expanded dramatically and its involvement in the everyday affairs of Americans became commonplace.

World War II

In the early days of World War II, the United States was committed to staying out of the conflict. While the advance of Nazi forces was disturbing, the events were taking place in Europe and did not directly affect Americans. Even when France was overrun in 1940 and the attacks on Great Britain intensified, the United States maintained its position of neutrality.

All of that changed on December 7, 1941 when the first wave of Japanese fighters began their assault on Pearl Harbor. By 9:45am, Honolulu time, the attack was over and 2,403 Americans had been killed. For the remainder of the day, FDR met with Congressional leaders and on December 8, the United States entered the second World War. The declaration of war against Japan prompted Germany and Italy to declare war against the United States a few days later so in less than a week, the United States had gone from neutrality to fighting a two-front war.[4]

Americans quickly mobilized as thousands of young men, including celebrities like William Holden and Jimmy Stewart, entered the armed forces. Those who were not in the military contributed to the war effort by planting "victory gardens", buying war bonds, and curtailing their use of scarce commodities. The Office of Price Administration was established and every man, woman, and child living in the United States was issued a ration book. By 1942, the number of items being rationed had grown and included sugar, coffee, rubber, and gasoline. Though some exceptions could be found, most Americans were committed to winning the war and were willing to make significant sacrifices for the greater good.[5]

For three more years, American forces battled the Axis powers until victory was achieved in 1945. When the Japanese surrendered on August 14, Americans celebrated the end of World War II and applauded the collective effort that had produced the victory. In the years immediately after the war, another reason to celebrate became apparent. The military buildup that was needed to fight the enemy had also lifted the United States out of the Depression.

A Snapshot of America: 1940

In 1940, the United States was becoming an urban society. The Depression and Dust Bowl had forced many farm families to abandon their homestead and move to more populated areas in search of employment. Nearly all of the children between the ages of seven and fourteen were in school but the percentage dropped for those in their later teenage years. Approximately 70% of sixteen and seventeen year olds were students but less than one in three eighteen and nineteen year olds continued their education. The number of Americans attending college was even lower with less than one in ten college-aged citizens pursuing a higher education. The value of formal education was growing but a high school diploma was still considered sufficient for most jobs.

One in four Americans were employed in the manufacturing sector with another 19% working in occupations related to agriculture, forestry, or fishing. A typical family had an annual income of less than a thousand dollars which was earned primarily by the man of the house. While some women were employed, the range of jobs available to them was very limited. Within a few years, however, the role of women in the labor force would expand dramatically. As men left the factories for military service, women filled the vacancies and "Rosie the Riveter" became instrumental in producing the items needed to support the war effort.[6]

Characteristics of the Generation

Builders were raised in this environment and have developed a generational perspective that reflects their shared experiences. A primary characteristic of the Builders is the way in which they have repeatedly sacrificed their personal desires for the good of the group. During the Depression years, many Builders left school prematurely in order to help their families pay the bills. During the later stages of World War II, Builders joined the armed forces and contributed to the victories in Europe and the Pacific. When civilian life resumed, Builders worked hard to provide opportunities for their children that had not been available to them. The common thread running through these events is the manner in which individual aspirations were placed behind the needs of the group.

Builders have also displayed a high degree of loyalty to the institutions and causes in which they have participated. The expression "company man" typifies many Builders since they spent their entire career with the same employer. In terms of their religious affiliation, Builders displayed a similar level of commitment. Rather than moving from one congregation to another, Builders became members of one church and remained loyal to it throughout their adult years. These behaviors are the reason why Builders were given their generational name. Through hard work and steadfast commitment, the United States was built into a global superpower in the years following World War II and the Builders were the driving force behind it.

Another characteristic of the Builders is their respect for authority which was instilled by their parents and thoroughly reinforced in the military. By the time Builders entered the highly bureaucratic working environments of post-war America they were intimately familiar with the vertical structure of organizations and the chain of command that accompanied them. Whether they agreed with the orders or not, Builders learned the importance of following the instructions given by their supervisors.

Perhaps the most visible trait of the Builders has been their thriftiness. Since their formative years occurred during the Great Depression and World War II, Builders learned the importance of being frugal early in life. The financial hardships and rationing of goods and services during this era deeply affected the Builders. When economic prosperity returned during the post-war years, Builders remembered the uncertain times which prompted them to save their money rather than spend it frivolously. Often this behavior is assumed to be the result of their age but in reality it is a product of their generational experience.

Builders now range in age from the early 60s to the late 70s which means 14% of the American population is a part of this generation. Due to their position in the life cycle, some Builders have retired from full-time work but others are still active participants in the labor force. Many churches are led by Builders since a large percentage of preaching ministers and elders are drawn from this generation. Occasionally, Builders are criticized for being too conservative or unwilling to change but when their generational perspective is considered, their actions are far more understandable.

Builders: An Illustration

On October 29, 1929, the stock market crashed. One day later, Ernest Clevenger, Jr. was born. The oldest of four children, Ernest and his siblings were raised in a God-fearing, hard-working family in Chattanooga, Tennessee. During the first ten years of his life, the Clevenger family faced severe economic challenges due to the Depression. At one point, Ernest's father earned $8 a week by delivering newspapers in the morning, selling blocks of ice from a mule-drawn wagon in the afternoon, and repairing crystal radio sets in the evening. Things began to change for Ernest and his family in 1940 when his father went to work in the stockroom of Corley Manufacturing, a company that produced and distributed saw mills. By the time of his retirement, Ernest's father had worked his way up the company ladder and eventually served as president and chairman of the board.

An avid reader and industrious young man, Ernest entered the business world at the age of 14 when he started a used bicycle shop with his brother and a neighborhood friend. The trio rented a garage for $1 a month where they assembled the parts they had purchased. After a coat of spray paint, the bicycles were sold and the young men enjoyed a respectable profit.

The work ethic that Ernest saw in his father and that he developed early in his life continued in his adult years. After attending David Lipscomb College from 1947 to 1951, Ernest entered full-time ministry. As a means of reaching out to members of his community, Ernest began writing newspaper articles that addressed topics of local interest. His success in this area led to other writing endeavors and in 1963 he published the first of 42 books he has written. During this time, he also attended graduate school where he earned two master's degrees and a doctorate degree in sacred literature.

Ernest's ability to handle challenging situations garnered the attention of Alabama Christian College (ACC) and in 1976 he accepted the position of academic dean. Following three and a half years with ACC, he moved to his hometown of Chattanooga to become the president of Boyd-Buchannan Christian School. During his tenure of nearly three years, enrollment rose from 534 to 804 students, athletic fields were built, and grant money from a foundation was secured for the first time in the school's history.

In 1982, Ernest returned to ACC as the president and began the process of moving the institution toward university status. For five years, Ernest helped to create Faulkner University and added colleges of business and law to the existing programs of study. Along the way, he dealt with a major crisis in the financial aid office by writing a bill that was passed by the United States Congress in 1986.

After his years at Faulkner, Ernest and his wife moved to Nashville in order to be closer to their son, daughter, and grandchildren. During his first year in Nashville, Ernest renovated the house they bought and started doing bookkeeping work for small companies. Soon thereafter, he created the Parchment Group which included the bookkeeping firm and a publishing business he had established in 1963. Eventually, he closed the bookkeeping firm but the publishing component became a subsidiary of Mid America Distributors where Ernest now serves as vice-president and corporate director.

The professional life of Ernest Clevenger has been characterized by building. Whether it was a local church, a school, or a business, he has poured his energy into the institutions and causes of which he has been a part. Ernest's work ethic, sacrificial spirit, and belief in the American Dream clearly illustrate the characteristics of his generation.

Summary

The golden era of post-war America was due, in large part, to the hard work and dedication of the Builders. Their commitment to building a better society than they had experienced during their formative years helped to make the United States a global superpower. Without diminishing their tremendous sacrifices and accomplishments, it can be argued that the most significant contribution of the Builders was their creation of the Baby Boomers. In Chapter 5, we will be introduced to America's largest and most powerful generation.

Chapter 5
Baby Boomers
(1946-1964)

For many Americans, the 1950s was a golden era of economic prosperity attributed to hard work, strong leadership, and the virtues of free enterprise. The majority of Americans were content with the status quo, firmly against communism, and reluctant to tamper with the system that seemed to be working so well. However, a Supreme Court decision in 1954 set in motion a monumental series of changes that would energize the Baby Boom generation for many years to come. In Brown vs. Board of Education, the Supreme Court ruled that separate but equal schools were unconstitutional. Two years later, the Court issued the Brown vs. Board of Education II ruling because so little had been done in response to the initial decision.

At the same time the courts were struggling to desegregate schools, grassroots efforts were underway to break down the system of discrimination that was so firmly in place in most southern states. In 1955, Rosa Parks refused to surrender her seat on a city bus to a white passenger. Her subsequent arrest sparked the Montgomery, Alabama bus boycott and brought a young minister, Dr. Martin Luther King, into prominence. With his charismatic leadership style and a philosophy of non-violent protest, the Montgomery city buses were eventually desegregated. Inspired by their accomplishment, African Americans expanded their efforts and sought change in other areas of society. As the struggle continued into the 1960s, a growing number of Boomers sympathized with their plight and desired to help. Throughout the South, committed volunteers worked tirelessly to ensure equal treatment for all citizens. Frequently, their efforts were rewarded with physical punishment, arrest and imprisonment, or both. As three young men learned during a 1964 voter registration campaign in Mississippi, involvement in the Civil Rights Movement could even lead to death.

As the struggle continued in the South, Betty Friedan added a new dimension to the quest for equal rights. In her 1963 book, *The Feminine Mystique*, Friedan questioned the limited opportunities that were available to women in the United States. During the 1950s, the majority of women had been housewives and those that were not had very few occupational choices. Friedan sought to change this and in 1966 she formed the National Organization for Women (NOW).[1] As membership in NOW increased, so did its impact on society. Using methods similar to those employed in the Civil Rights Movement, NOW worked to alter America's view of women while creating educational and employment opportunities that had not existed before.

While the Civil Rights and Women's Liberation Movements received a great deal of attention because of their focus on pressing domestic issues, the struggle against the spread of communism in Southeast Asia seemed far away both geographically and emotionally. However, as the 1960s progressed, the war in Vietnam escalated and so did the opposition to it. The outcry against involvement in the war seemed to galvanize the Boomers and gave them a cause into which they could pour their collective energy. A counterculture movement was already underway and fighting a war that was seen as having limited relevance to the United States only intensified the anti-establishment sentiment among many young Americans. Despite being raised in a time when institutional loyalty, conformity, and respect for authority were heavily emphasized, a sizeable number of Boomers discarded these values and replaced them with a new set that emphasized personal freedom, self expression, and instant gratification. Protests against the Vietnam War, the draft, and anything associated with "the establishment" became regular events, especially on college campuses, as young people openly questioned decisions made by those in positions of authority.

Music Set the Tone

In 1951, disc jockey Alan Freed began playing Rhythm and Blues (R&B) music from his Cleveland, Ohio radio station.[2] Recognizing that R&B was a musical genre closely associated with the African American community, Freed changed the name to Rock 'n' Roll in order to appeal to a larger audience. The strong signal of his station spread throughout the Midwest and exposed thousands of young people to the music of artists like Little Richard and Chuck Berry.

The popularity of Rock 'n' Roll increased rapidly as listeners were attracted to the energizing sound and distinctive beat of the music. Nevertheless, a problem

existed. While a few artists were white, the majority of
Rock 'n' Roll music was performed by African Americans.
At a time when segregation was firmly in place in many
areas of the country, promoting African American artists
to white listeners was a formidable challenge. Sam
Phillips, the owner of Sun Records, was keenly aware of
this dilemma and was anxious to find a "white man with
a Negro sound."[3] In 1956, he did. Elvis Presley, the
son of a poor Mississippi family, came to Sun Records
and recorded "Heartbreak Hotel." On April 21, 1956 it
topped the Billboard chart and transformed the music
industry. For 55 of the next 100 weeks, Elvis had the
best selling record in America with hits like "Hound
Dog", "Love Me Tender", and "Don't Be Cruel."[4]

Elvis' grip on Rock 'n' Roll seemed to be insurmountable
even during his absence for military service. In the early
1960s, however, the British Invasion began and the Beatles
attracted a cult-like following. Their first hit, "I Want to
Hold Your Hand", sold three million copies in less than
a month but Beatle Mania extended far beyond record
sales.[5] Hair styles, clothes, vocabulary, and belief systems
changed as a result of the group and their music. For
instance, the mop-looking hair style worn by the Beatles
became very popular following their first appearance in
the United States. Later, their participation in Eastern
religions introduced a new set of religious possibilities to
individuals who had been raised in the Judeo-Christian
tradition. One of the leaders of the group, John Lennon,
even staged a highly publicized anti-war protest from his
bedroom as he declared that Americans should make
love not war.

The behavior of artists like Elvis and the Beatles
raised serious concerns over the effects that Rock 'n'

Roll music was having in America. For years, adults had worried that Rock 'n' Roll was negatively influencing American youth and causing them to discard the values they had been taught.[6] Teenagers assured their parents that Rock 'n' Roll was just music and they really weren't being changed by it but in retrospect, the adults were correct. Rock 'n' Roll became a major mechanism through which Baby Boomers expressed their discontent with American society. Initially, the lyrics were fairly benign but the actions of the performers pushed the boundaries of decency. The on-stage gyrations of Elvis and Little Richard were considered to be offensive by adults though young people viewed them as a refreshing break from 1950s conformity. By the 1960s, the message became more important as artists used their music to comment on events that were significant to Boomers like the Vietnam War, sexual freedom, the evils of capitalism, and the student deaths at Kent State University.

Boomer Religion

Boomers were raised in a very religious era. Throughout their formative years, the majority of Boomers went to church, said grace before meals, and recited a prayer at the beginning of the school day.

As they became young adults, there was every indication that this pattern would continue. However, during the 1960s, a sizeable number of Boomers abandoned their religious roots and embarked on a spiritual journey that led them through various forms of Christianity and a number of world religions. The departure of some Boomers from their religious moorings was expected since it is common for young people to leave their religious roots for a brief period of time. In the case of the Boomers, however, the exodus from mainline churches was massive and many have still not returned.

In an effort to understand their religious behavior, Wade Clark Roof has studied the Boomers in great depth and has identified three religious subcultures that describe them.[7] First, some Boomers are *loyalists*. While many of their peers left the church, loyalists remained. As a group, they never identified with the counterculture of the 1960s and generally had positive interactions with their parent's generation. In contrast, *dropouts* left the church in groves and were deeply involved in the counterculture. From their perspective, religious institutions were out of touch with the values and lifestyles of their generation and had little to offer them. Roof's third group, *returnees*, fits between loyalists and dropouts. Their views were not as extreme as the dropouts yet they were dissatisfied with institutional religion. After searching for alternative belief systems, returnees eventually found their way back to organized religion often because of the birth of their own children and a desire to instill religious values in them.

While dropouts have maintained their distance from institutional religion, loyalists and returnees are now exerting a significant influence on churches. Because they are willing to embrace a wide range of non-traditional beliefs and practices, Boomers are often considered to be less religious than previous generations which can create tension among the members. In reality, the Boomers are very interested in spiritual growth and development but they want the worship service to be conducted in a manner that is culturally relevant to them.

A Snapshot of America: 1960

By 1960, the population of the United States had grown to 179 million due in large part to the post-war baby boom. From 1946 to 1953, the number of births steadily increased but between 1954 and 1964, they skyrocketed. More than four million babies were born each year during that span including 4.2 million in 1960.[8]

The majority of Boomers were born to married couples who lived in urban or suburban areas. If siblings were not already in place, they were likely to follow. The family was supported primarily by the father though a growing number of women were entering the labor force in clerical or service positions. Eight out of ten American families made less than $10,000 annually and half earned less than $6,000 per year.[9]

Noticeably absent from the labor force were children and adolescents. Since inflation was low and stable employment in the manufacturing sector was available, it was possible for a family to live reasonably well on one income. Young people were not required to contribute to the financial well-being of the family as had been the case earlier in the 20th century. Instead, they were expected to focus on formal education and prepare themselves for college admission and then entrance into a labor force that increasingly consisted of white-collar occupations.

Characteristics of the Generation

Raised in this environment, Boomers developed a generational perspective that was unlike those of their parents or grandparents. From a very early age, Boomers were showered with attention. Since the childhood of many Builders had been interrupted by the Depression and World War II, they worked extremely hard to provide a stable setting in which the Boomers could thrive. A premium was placed on families spending time together and the children were usually at the center of the interaction.

At the same time, community planners and marketing executives recognized the enormous size of the Boomers and the need to respond to them. Building affordable housing for the ever increasing number of young families became a high priority for many communities. Soon thereafter, the construction of classrooms and playgrounds increased as Boomers prepared to enter elementary school. Businesses saw a burgeoning market in the Boomers and began to develop new products and services designed specifically for them. Throughout the process, Boomers were constantly being asked what they liked and disliked. The result of this high level of attention was that they developed a strong sense of entitlement. For as long as Boomers could remember, the world had revolved around them and they were accustomed to being the center of attention.

When the 1960s began, the leading-edge Boomers were preparing to enter adulthood and Americans were confident that the instruction they had received in family, school, and church settings would manifest itself in positive ways. Initially, that expectation was correct. In 1961, the Peace Corp was formed by President Kennedy and Boomers quickly embraced it because they believed they could change the world. As the decade progressed, however, a growing number of Boomers turned away from the values they had been taught and began to emphasize their individuality. Life in the post-war years had placed a premium on conforming to group expectations and

Boomers were constantly being reminded of what was expected of them in terms of appearance, beliefs, and lifestyle. By the mid 1960s, a dramatic shift was underway as Boomers saw inconsistencies between the values that were espoused in America and the reality that existed. In response, many rejected the values they had been taught and replaced them with a "live for the moment" mentality. Everything was subject to scrutiny including the role of government, the virtues of capitalism, and the whole notion of authority.

During the 1970s, most of the Boomers returned to the mainstream of society but they brought with them a strong emphasis on individualism and a willingness to think outside of the box. Their view of marriage, parenting, religion, and work continued to challenge the existing social structure and their tendency to go to the extremes gave birth to the "yuppie" movement of the 1980s.

Boomers now occupy positions of significant influence in schools, businesses, government, and churches and their propensity to think and act in unconventional ways remains in place though it has been tempered somewhat by age. As a group, Boomers continue to look for ways to apply the principles they believe in to the groups and causes in which they participate even if it means challenging the status quo. In terms of their religious habits, Boomers have been referred to as a "generation of seekers" who participate in a "spiritual marketplace."[10] Dissatisfied with the range of religious offerings available to them, Boomers have combined belief systems that seem to be contradictory into individualized religions and they have been at the forefront of the non-denominational church movement. Both of these activities illustrate that

Boomers continue to display a willingness to go outside of the established boundaries in order to apply their perspective.

Baby Boomers: An Illustration

His resume is impressive and includes a bachelor's degree in Bible, a master's degree in divinity, a master's degree in American history, and significant progress on a doctorate degree in history. In terms of practical experience, he ministered for more than twenty years with churches in Louisiana and Texas before accepting his current position. With credentials such as these, it would be reasonable to assume that Larry James is a faculty member at a university or is the preaching minister for a large, metropolitan church. Instead, Larry is the Executive Director of Central Dallas Ministries (CDM) which began as a grassroots effort to empower individuals and build a sense of community in a poor neighborhood in East Dallas.

Born in the state of Washington in 1950, Larry's family moved to Richardson, Texas in 1953 to be closer to their extended family and with the hope of finding a place where they could settle and raise their son. Throughout his formative years, Larry was deeply affected by the social injustice he saw around him. As part of a mowing crew that maintained the parks and athletic fields in Richardson, he worked with a number of African American individuals and gained an appreciation for the difficulties they experienced due to the color of their skin. On one occasion, the crew went to a convenience store to buy a soft drink but only the white workers were allowed to enter the store. This experience was seared into Larry's memory and would resurface years later.

When he graduated from Richardson High School in 1968, Larry attended Harding College in Searcy, Arkansas and then attended the Harding Graduate School of Religion until 1973 when he accepted a full-time position with a church in Shreveport, Louisiana. Though Larry gained valuable experience during his two years in Shreveport, he also encountered blatant racism in the church which deeply disturbed him and led to his decision to leave. In 1975, he moved his family to New Orleans in order to minister with the Carrollton Avenue Church of Christ. An urban church located two blocks from Canal Street, Larry's experience with the Carrollton Avenue congregation afforded him a unique blend of street people, pimps, and fortune tellers along with many members who had been raised in the Church of Christ.

After five years in New Orleans, Larry had the opportunity to return to the Richardson East Church of Christ were he had served as a youth minister in the early 1970s. With his compassion for hurting people and commitment to social justice, Larry encouraged the Richardson East congregation to reach out to the disenfranchised in the community. His vision led to the formation of a food pantry, numerous 12-step programs, and a congregation where individuals with AIDS were welcomed. It also garnered the attention of CDM. When Larry was asked to become the Executive Director of CDM, he was reluctant but eventually accepted the position and joined a small staff that ran a food pantry and walk-in clinic in an economically depressed neighborhood in East Dallas. Larry's early work with CDM lacked a clear vision but over time he realized that, rather than just distributing groceries, CDM needed to empower individuals and encourage them to be active participants in building their community.

Today, CDM has an annual operating budget of 3.9 million dollars, a staff of sixty four people, and a database with more than 500 volunteers most of whom receive services from CDM. From its humble beginnings as a food pantry and small church, CDM has grown to include legal services, a medical and dental clinic, after-school and summer programs, workforce development and technical centers, a Federal Credit Union, and a community development corporation. In addition, the success of CDM has gained the attention of civic leaders, researchers, and celebrities such as Bill Cosby.

Due to the widespread recognition that CDM receives, Larry has had the opportunity to speak at numerous events around the country, work with nationally renowned scholars, and even consider the possibility of running for public office at the local or state level. While the accolades are nice and the future seems full of new opportunities, Larry remains focused on the people in East Dallas and the principles of compassion and social justice.

Summary

As the largest and most powerful generation of the 20th century, Boomers have had an enormous impact on society. Their movement through the life cycle has led to the transformation of families, schools, and churches. Given the scope of their influence, Boomers have become the standard against which other generations are measured. As we will see in Chapter 6, members of Generation X have not always embraced this evaluation.

Chapter 6
Generation X
(1965-1983)

One of the most significant developments in the history of the United States occurred in 1971 but very few Americans realized it. Ted Hoff, an employee at Intel, was able to place all of the elements needed to run a computer on a single silicon chip. While computers had been a part of the American experience since 1946 when the 30 ton ENIAC machine first appeared, most citizens had no idea what a computer was and very little interest in obtaining one. Hoff's microprocessor did little to change the view of the common man but it fascinated a group of science and math enthusiasts in Menlo Park, California. In 1975, the Homebrew Computer Club was formed due in large part to the possibilities that the microprocessor presented. Working out of their basements and garages, the diverse collection of hackers and pioneers shared their inventions with one another and envisioned a day when computers would revolutionize every aspect of life in the United States.

Among the members of the Homebrew Club were Steve Wozniak and Steve Jobs. The more technically-inclined of the two, Wozniak developed the Apple I computer in 1976 primarily for his own enjoyment and that of his friends. Upon seeing the machine, Jobs saw a business opportunity and began to promote the Apple I. Unfortunately, the market for personal computers was extremely small and the initial efforts met with limited success. In 1981, however, computer giant IBM released a personal computer and interest in the new device soared. As IBM struggled to support the demand it had created, Wozniak and Jobs continued working on a graphics-oriented computer that involved clicking on icons with a "mouse" rather than writing programs. By the end of 1983, the MacIntosh was ready to be launched and millions of Americans gained access to a user-friendly personal computer.[1]

Seeing the World

Channel 17 was the epitome of mediocrity until Ted Turner purchased it in 1970. Using a program format of reruns, movies, and Atlanta Braves baseball games, Turner transformed the lowly station into a cable television giant. As the scope of TBS grew, Turner's attention shifted to creating a 24-hour news channel. Though skeptics abounded, Turner launched the Cable News Network in 1980 and when the Gulf War began a decade later it was CNN that delivered real-time audio and video from the front line.

While Ted Turner was revolutionizing television news, MTV was reshaping the music industry. When it began in 1981, MTV was aimed primarily at teenagers and a number of new artists were introduced since videos were not the norm among established performers. Within a few years, record company executives recognized the marketing power that videos provided and the influence of MTV grew. For most artists, releasing an album or cassette was only part of the process. In order to appeal to the widest audience possible, it was necessary to create a video of their music, as well.

The emphasis on visual presentations swept through the recording industry but it did not stop there. Newspapers, the bastion of the printed word, also experienced a significant transformation. When USA Today first appeared in 1982, its owners envisioned a daily newspaper that could compete with televised news programs. In order to accomplish that, they would have to depart from industry standards and create a document that was more appealing to a wider audience. The result was a paper saturated with photos and graphics along with shorter stories that were crisply written. The general public loved the new format but critics of USA Today said they had done to the newspaper what McDonalds had done to the dining experience.[2]

From 1980 to 1982, the bar was raised for news and entertainment providers. Consumers, particularly those who were young, were no longer satisfied with hearing a song, reading a black and white newspaper, or becoming aware of major events after they occurred. They wanted information presented to them quickly, concisely, and in a visual form. Whether CNN, MTV, and USA Today created this desire or simply responded to it is unclear but a new set of expectations was firmly in place.

Body Art

When the punk rock movement began in the late 1970s, members of the mainstream culture were amazed by what they saw. In an effort to establish a unique identity and to protest the alienation they felt, punk rockers went to great lengths to alter their appearance. One of the most shocking manifestations of their desire was the manner in which they pierced their skin with safety pins. It was not uncommon to see at least one ordinary safety pin dangling from the lip or eyebrow of a punk rocker. Inspired by the rebellious display, other artists and musicians quickly followed suit.[3]

At approximately the same time, a renewed interest in tattooing emerged. Though tattoos had long been associated with sailors, prisoners, and gang members, more colorful and original designs began to appear in the late 70s and early 80s. The combination of piercings and tattoos became known as "body art" and provided an excellent opportunity for self-expression. Adolescents were particularly smitten by what they thought was a new idea but they failed to realize that body art had been commonly seen for centuries across many cultures. For instance, archaeologists discovered a 2,400 year old mummy from Russia with a tattoo on her bicep and Victorian era royalty in England were known to have pierced various parts of their body.[4] Nevertheless, the popularity of body art continued to grow and even members of the mainstream culture began to tattoo and pierce their bodies.

Though accurate numbers are difficult to determine, it is estimated that between seven and twenty million adults have participated in the body art phenomenon.[5] In addition to ears, which are the most commonly pierced area, body art enthusiasts have also developed an affinity for piercing the nose, tongue, naval, and other less visible parts of the human anatomy.

A Snapshot of America: 1980

By 1980, the population of the United States had grown to slightly more than 226 million and nearly three out of every four Americans lived in an urban area. The movement away from rural areas is clearly illustrated when one considers that the number of urban dwellers in 1980 was greater than the entire population in 1920. Thirty percent of Americans made their living in technical, sales, or administrative support positions while an additional 23% worked in managerial or professional specialty occupations. In other words, more than half of employed Americans were white collar workers who relied on their formal education as much as their physical strength. Approximately one in five worked in blue collar positions such as machine operators, fabricators, or laborers and less than 3% of the population earned a living through farming, forestry, or fishing.

The role of formal education was quite pronounced as 88% of Americans between the ages of sixteen and seventeen were enrolled in school. While the figure was comparable to school enrollment in 1970 and 1960, it was significantly larger than in the first half of the century. Only 70% of Americans between the ages of sixteen and seventeen were enrolled in school in 1940 and less than half of that age group was enrolled in 1920. The rise in formal education was accompanied by an increase in annual family income. By 1980, 35% of families had an annual income of $25,000 or more and less than 10% of the population lived below the poverty level established by the federal government.

A growing number of young adults opted to postpone marriage until later in life. Among those who were fifteen years of age or older, one in four females and three out of every ten males were single. While a partial explanation for these figures is the presence of divorced or widowed adults, it also reflects an extension of the formal education process. Rather than graduating from high school, getting married, and entering the labor force, a growing number of Americans entered college and delayed making long-term commitments to marriage or employment.[6]

Characteristics of the Generation

Members of Generation X have been called a number of things and most of them are not flattering. Cynical, pessimistic, and apathetic are among the adjectives that have been used to describe the generation that grew up in the wake of the Baby Boomers.[7] Many GenXers were raised in either a single parent or a dual-income family which meant that they spent an inordinate amount of time away from the influence of their parent or parents.[8] In order to develop a sense of belonging and direction, GenXers turned to their peers and to television. It is not a coincidence that one of the most popular television shows during the 1990s was "Friends" which focused on a group of GenXers trying to navigate their way through life by relying on one another rather than members of their parent's generation. The result of this experience is that GenXers have also been referred to as the "lonely generation" which led to the development of deep friendships with individuals in their immediate vicinity.[9] While the internet has given them access to the world, many GenXers feel a very strong allegiance to their local community and the friends who helped them navigate the uncertainties that accompanied their formative years.

Since the maturation of Generation X and the rise of the personal computer coincided, GenXers have developed a heavy reliance on technology in nearly every aspect of their life. They expect to receive information in real time through the World Wide Web and electronic mail. In addition, they are an extremely visual generation that wants graphics and pictures to accompany the written or spoken word. Publishers, educators, and even ministers have had to alter the manner in which they present material due to the expectations that GenXers have brought to society. Even the most articulate lecture or well written book will only be of modest interest to GenXers unless it includes Power Point slides or other visual aids.

Another characteristic of Generation X is that there are very few absolutes in their view of the world which, in large part, is a product of the postmodern era in which they have lived (see Chapter 2). Since one of the fundamental tenants of postmodernism is that truth is relative, one set of beliefs is considered to be as true as another. While this approach does lead to a more pluralistic society, it also encourages the development of a moral vacuum in which nothing is absolute and all belief systems are considered to be equally valid.

This view impacts the vocational outlook of GenXers. While they are the most highly educated group in American history, whether GenXers will experience the economic prosperity enjoyed by the Builders and Boomers is unclear.[10] The notion that higher education and hard work are the prerequisites to the good life has been questioned by GenXers based on what they have witnessed. Though their parents experienced financial success, the long hours at work and steadfast commitment to career advancement had a negative impact on many of their personal relationships. In addition, GenXers witnessed an endless series of scandals involving junk-bond dealers, politicians, and even religious leaders. To them, the future is uncertain and pre-determined formulas for success are of little value.

The propensity of GenXers to question the existence of absolute truth also impacts their religious behavior. Many GenXers were not exposed to organized religion when they were young so when they first encounter a church that teaches the existence of "one Lord, one faith, one baptism" (Eph. 4:5) they tend to be very skeptical. However, if a church allows them to explore their new surroundings and ask questions, even if they seem to be irreverent, then the initial resistance may well subside. Many GenXers are attracted to the structure and authority that a church can provide since those qualities were often in short supply during their childhood and teenage years.[11] The development of intimate friendships, often through participation in small group activities, is also very appealing to GenXers because it provides a sense of belonging reminiscent of the relationships they have established in other areas of their life.[12]

Generation X: An Illustration

Devoid of body art and the grunge look, Steve McQuirk defies the stereotypes attached to Generation X. At a deeper level, though, Steve's perspective on life has been shaped by the experiences he has shared with his contemporaries. Born in 1967 in Leavenworth, Kansas, Steve's parents divorced when he was two. While he continued to spend time with his father, Steve and his siblings were raised primarily by their mother who balanced a full-time job with her parental responsibilities.

Money was always an issue in their household so when it came time to consider college, Steve knew that he would have to finance his own education. After learning that the military academies provided an all-expenses paid education, Steve began the long process of seeking admission to one of the schools. When he was offered an opportunity to attend the Air Force Academy, Steve eagerly accepted and during his time in Colorado Springs he developed a desire to become a pilot.

Following his graduation in 1989, Steve made a ten year commitment to the Air Force in exchange for extensive pilot's training. While stationed in California, he met Jenny Cullins and the two developed a strong friendship that led to their marriage in 1994. A fundamental part of their relationship was a desire to serve the Lord so they joined a large Presbyterian church that had an extensive small group ministry. Steve was familiar with organized religion since his maternal grandparents had introduced him to Christianity early in life but during his adolescent and early adult years he had not maintained a relationship with God. The opportunity to participate in a small group ministry provided an ideal way for Steve to re-establish his commitment to Christ. When they were transferred to Wichita, Kansas immediately after their wedding, Steve and Jenny visited several churches before locating a non-denominational church that also emphasized small group settings.

After six years in Kansas, the couple moved to Texas so Steve could fly for a major airline based in Dallas. For three years, Steve paid his dues and gradually worked his way up among the company's pilots. During this time, however, the airline industry began to change and the number of pilots needed by the major carriers declined. The events of September 11, 2001 intensified the changing nature of the industry and despite his education at the Air Force Academy, extensive training in the military, and level of experience, Steve was furloughed. Eventually he was hired by another airline but Steve's career path is a vivid illustration of why many GenXers question whether they will experience the same level of vocational and economic opportunity that their parents and grandparents enjoyed.

Summary

Living in the shadow of the Baby Boomers has not been an easy task. GenXers have struggled to establish their own identity and separate themselves from the endless comparisons with the Boomers. The popularity of body art among GenXers is one way in which they have provided a visible distinction between themselves and the preceding generation. Despite the frequent criticism of their appearance and apparent lack of initiative, GenXers are perfectly willing to invest their energy in authentic relationships and worthwhile causes. A prime example of that can be seen in the way they have showered their own children with attention. As we will see in Chapter 7, GenXers have been actively involved in the lives of the Millennials.

Chapter 7
Millennials
(1984-2002)

When William Bennett began his tenure as Secretary of Education in 1985, the public education system in the United States was in shambles. A few years earlier, the National Commission on Excellence in Education had been formed to examine the condition of public schools and when they released their report, Americans were both stunned and outraged. In "A Nation at Risk", the Commission reported that functional illiteracy was alarmingly high, math and science scores had steadily declined since the 1960s, and most college graduates were only marginally prepared to enter the increasingly sophisticated labor force. The Commission expressed deep concerns about the future of the United States unless high quality public education became a priority for elected officials, school administrators, parents, and children.[1]

In response to the grim report, the arduous task of rebuilding America's public school system began and William Bennett was at the forefront of the effort. One of the first areas to be overhauled was the curriculum. Concerned that students were not being taught a sufficient number of core courses, a "Back to Basics" philosophy was adopted in schools across the nation. A heavy emphasis was placed on math, science, reading, and writing often at the expense of elective courses. Subjects that were not considered to be absolutely essential to a student's academic achievement were eliminated in order to focus on the basic curriculum.

In the midst of this struggle, Bennett was a strong proponent of character education. He believed that values such as responsibility, self-discipline, courage, and honesty had a place in the curriculum and could be effectively taught by emphasizing classical literature. Though his vision did not fully materialize while he served as Secretary of Education, it did gain national prominence during the 1990s. Beginning with "The Book of Virtues" and later "The Book of Virtues for Young People" and the "Children's Book of Virtues", Bennett emphasized the need for families and schools to teach America's young people about the importance of good character.

At approximately the same time, accountability became the buzz word in educational circles. While achievement tests had been used for a number of years to measure the progress of individual students, a new form of assessment emerged. The public wanted to know how schools were performing. A set of criteria and terminology was established so that parents could know whether their child was attending an "exemplary" school or one that was not meeting the minimum requirements established by the state board of education. Standardized testing became a major mechanism by which schools and students were evaluated.

The effort to improve schools extended beyond the classroom. In response to growing concerns about the use of drugs by children and adolescents, schools developed "drug free zones" around their campus. Individuals possessing or trying to distribute drugs on school grounds were subject to expulsion, prosecution, or both. In addition, students who wanted to participate in extracurricular activities were required to pass a drug test in order to ensure that they were not using illegal substances.

"Gun free zones" also appeared near schools. The growth of street gangs and the more violent nature of the crimes that were being committed by juveniles concerned school administrators and led to the development of strict policies that prohibited the possession of weapons on a school campus. In order to enforce the new rules, metal detectors were installed at many schools and students began their day by walking through them and having their backpacks or purses searched by security personnel.

Terror and Terrorists

Modifications to the curriculum and strict enforcement of campus safety policies led to a noticeable improvement in the educational system. The increased level of accountability and "zero tolerance" approach to student behavior seemed to produce a safer and more focused learning environment but the stability of the new order was severely challenged in the late 1990s. Over an eighteen month span extending from October of 1997 to April of 1999, twelve separate school shootings occurred as disgruntled students smuggled weapons onto campus and opened fire on their classmates and teachers.[2]

One of the earliest attacks took place in Pearl, Mississippi when a 17 year old student stabbed his mother to death and then took a rifle to school. When his assault ended, two students were killed and seven others were wounded. Exactly two months later, a 14 year old boy in West Paducah, Kentucky fired into a group of students who had gathered before school for an informal prayer service killing three and wounding five.[3]

In March of the following year, a 13 year old boy and his 11 year old cousin ambushed teachers and students at a middle school in Jonesboro, Arkansas. After activating the school's fire alarm, the two boys retreated to a wooded area behind the school where their weapons had been stashed. As teachers led their students out of the building, the attackers began firing into the crowd of people. When it finally ended, four students and one teacher had been killed.[4]

Approximately one year later, two teenagers wearing black trench coats entered Columbine High School in Littleton, Colorado with an arsenal of weapons. The assailants terrified students and teachers as they systematically moved through the building. After killing thirteen people and wounding twenty three others, the siege ended when the gunmen took their own lives.[5]

As the horror of the school shootings became known, shock and disbelief spread across the United States. The terror that had been inflicted on children was considered to be unacceptable and steps were taken to prevent it from happening again. In the midst of this effort, an attack occurred that threatened Americans of all ages. On September 11, 2001, two hijacked airplanes were flown into the World Trade Center Towers while another plane crashed into the Pentagon. A fourth airplane had been hijacked and was headed for Washington, D.C. but crashed near Pittsburgh, Pennsylvania when passengers battled the terrorists who had seized control of the aircraft. Nearly 3,000 lives were lost that day and the war on terrorism began soon thereafter.[6] For those who had experienced the attack on Pearl Harbor in 1941, the events of September 11 were hauntingly familiar.

A Snapshot of America: 2000

An analysis of the 2000 Census shows that Millennials were part of an increasingly diverse population. When the 20th century began, life expectancy was 47 years and only 4% of Americans were 65 years of age or older. By the end of the century, life expectancy had grown to 77 years and more than 12% of the population had passed the age of 65. The "age wave" and the "graying of America" became common expressions to describe the demographic shift and concerns about generational equity began to surface.

The racial composition of the population was also changing as the flow of immigrants from Latin America and Asia increased. While Anglo Americans continued to be the largest group followed by African Americans, a growing number of households were headed by an immigrant. The result was that in 17% of American homes the primary means of communicating was with a language other than English.

The size of the American family was being altered, as well. Though the number of babies born between 1984 and 2002 was similar to that of the Baby Boom years, the newborns were spread across a greater number of families. As a result, the average family size declined to 3.14 which meant that many Millennials were an only child. Interestingly, some of those children were actually raised by their grandparents. Close to six million grandparents lived in the same household as their grandchildren and 42% were responsible for raising them.

The importance of higher education continued to grow even though a college degree did not provide the same level of opportunity it had in the past. As access to higher education increased through on-line degree programs, more and more Americans became college students. Among those 25 years of age and older, nearly one out of every four possessed at least a bachelor's degree and many were pursuing graduate degrees in order to have a competitive advantage in the job market.[7]

Characteristics of the Generation

Like GenXers, Millennials are technologically-savvy, interested in spending time with their friends, and extremely visual.[8] Beyond that, the similarities begin to fade. While Millennials do participate in the body art craze that GenXers helped to popularize, they do so in a more modest way. Piercings and tattoos adorn the bodies of many Millennials but they are more discreetly placed and are seen as a form of decoration and self-expression rather than a statement against society.[9] The clothing choices of Millennials also are more acceptable to members of the mainstream culture as the "grunge" look has gradually disappeared.

Millennials possess an optimistic outlook that considers higher education to be the path to a promising career.[10] While they are aware that the cost of higher education has skyrocketed and a greater number of people are competing for admission to the most prestigious schools, they remain steadfast in their belief that a college education is absolutely essential for a successful career. As the number of Americans earning a bachelor's degree increases, Millennials also recognize that earning a graduate degree may be necessary to distance themselves from the crowd and provide the career opportunities they envision.

As a part of the most diverse population in American history, many Millennials count among their circle of friends individuals whose ancestry is traced to a nation other than the United States. In addition, one out of every five Millennials has at least one immigrant parent which means they have been raised in culturally diverse families.[11] As they begin to date and consider marriage partners, Millennials will be more likely than previous generations to consider marrying someone from a different racial or ethnic group.

The most striking feature of Millennials is the degree to which teamwork characterizes their endeavors.[12] Millennials are displaying a very collaborative approach to solving the challenges they encounter and they seem to be particularly interested in applying this method to civic affairs. Throughout the 1990s, many schools initiated service learning courses which awarded academic credit to students who participated in community service projects. As a result, Millennials have a higher degree of civic awareness and are more interested in the political process than GenXers were during their teenage years.

In terms of religion, faith is very important to Millennials but their allegiance is not to an institution. Millennials are deeply loyal to the people they trust and they place a premium on authentic relationships. As they consider whether to join a community of faith, a primary concern of Millennials is the degree to which they consider the members and their actions to be genuine.[13]

Millennials: An Illustration

During his sophomore year in high school, Robin Crocker participated in three projects that continue to shape his academic and professional goals. The first was a mock trial sponsored by a group of attorneys in his hometown of Sherman, Texas. Over a five month span, the group met three times a week (including Saturday morning) to learn the intricacies of the legal system and how it played out in the courtroom. At the same time, Robin became a member of his high school debate team which gave him the opportunity to sharpen his presentation skills and develop a more complete understanding of current events in the United States and abroad. Robin also became involved in Key Club which is a student organization closely associated with the Kiwanis Club. As a member, he learned the importance of civic responsibility by volunteering for a number of community enhancement projects.

As he entered his senior year in high school, Robin began to think seriously about college and explored the possibility of attending highly prestigious schools such as the University of Texas and Columbia University. He eventually decided to attend Harding University due to its strong religious emphasis and the positive experience he had during a campus visit. Initially, Robin declared his major to be public administration because of a deep interest in civic affairs and community building but later changed his major to political science with a minor in English due to a growing interest in the political process and his love of literature.

Robin's desire to make a difference in his community has strengthened during his time at Harding. While he enjoys college life and the casual interactions that take place among his circle of friends, Robin takes time out of his schedule to be of service to others. Along with a group of his peers, Robin volunteers at a homeless shelter on Friday nights and is actively involved in a prison ministry.

After completing his bachelor's degree, Robin plans to attend law school and focus on international law so that he can assist third world nations with their economic and community development. While he realizes that a career in law can be very lucrative, he is motivated by a strong desire to serve the common good and to help those who are in need.

Summary

Since the oldest Millennials are just beginning to reach adulthood, it is possible that their perspective will be modified in the coming years. Nevertheless, the information that is available at this time suggests that Millennials are approaching life with a degree of seriousness and steadfastness that resembles the perspective Builders had when they were young. Whether these characteristics are permanent remains to be seen but the Millennial perspective does appear to be noticeably different from that of Generation X.

Understanding Millennials, as well as the preceding generations, is essential for any group that wants to work with multiple generations but for a church the knowledge must be used in a manner consistent with God's will. In Chapter 8, we will turn our attention to a Biblical view of generations.

Chapter 8
A Biblical Perspective on Generations

Each of the languages in which the Bible was originally written has a word that is translated into English as "generation". In the Old Testament, dor (Hebrew) and dar (Aramaic) are used while genea (Greek) is the New Testament equivalent. While the terms do not specify the number of years a generation covers, they are used in multiple ways. For instance, Isaiah 51:9 and Colossians 1:26 describe the condition of previous generations while Isaiah 34:17 and Luke 1:48 refer to the future state of a generation. In Deuteronomy 32:5, Moses describes the Israelites as a "warped and crooked generation" due to their inconsistent loyalty to God while Jesus characterizes the crowd that was following him as being an "unbelieving and perverse generation" in Luke 9:41.[1]

A second Hebrew word, toledot, is closely connected to the previous terms but is more commonly used in genealogical lists. The Bible provides approximately twenty four genealogies, the first of which appears in Genesis chapter four. The purpose of genealogies was to establish a line of descent which provided an identity for an individual. This was particularly significant in three settings. First, only descendants of Levi could serve as priests (Numbers 1:50). Second, in the Southern kingdom, the descendants of David were the ones who sat on the throne (I Kings 2:1-4). Third, and most importantly, Matthew and Luke both provide the genealogy of Jesus by tracing his descent from David, Abraham, and Adam (Matt. 1:1-17; Luke 3:23-38).[2]

While the words "generation" or "generations" appear more than 200 times in the Bible,[3] eight sections of Scripture are reviewed in this chapter because they provide the depth of information needed to appreciate God's plan for his people. All quotations are taken from the New International Version.

Deuteronomy

Moses was an old man when he spoke the words that are recorded in the book of Deuteronomy. The nation of Israel was ready to enter the promised land but before they took possession of it, Moses called them together in order to recount their history. As he looked across the crowd that gathered, he realized that most of them had never been slaves in Egypt, walked through the Red Sea on dry ground, or received God's law at Mt. Sinai. Moses was speaking to a new generation and it was vitally important that he connect them to their heritage, to those who had gone before them, and to the covenant relationship that God had established with them.

The sixth chapter focuses specifically on the law that God had given and the significance of communicating it to subsequent generations. Beginning in verse four, the Bible says:

> Hear, O Israel! The Lord our God, the Lord is one! Love the Lord your God with all your heart and with all your soul and with all your strength.

These commandments that I give you today are to be upon your heart. Impress them on your children. Talk about them when you sit at home and when you walk along the road, when you lie down and when you get up.

Moses continues the exhortation in verse 20:

In the future, when your son asks you, "What is the meaning of the stipulations, decrees and laws the Lord our God has commanded you?" tell him: "We were slaves of Pharaoh in Egypt, but the Lord brought us out of Egypt with a mighty hand.

A precedent was set early in the history of Israelites. Older generations were given the responsibility of transmitting their faith to the generations that followed them. Certainly, this was to occur in formal settings but it was also expected that it would be a part of their everyday activities.

Judges

After the Israelites had settled into the land of Canaan, Joshua died and a new form of leadership was instituted. Though God would eventually yield to the Israelites' demand for an earthly king (I Samuel 8:6-7), in the interim he established a system of judges. Unlike its 20th century usage, in the Old Testament a judge was seen as being a deliverer. Rather than handing out punishment to the Israelites, the primary role of a judge was to accept God's calling and rescue the people from the enemy that was oppressing them due to their unfaithfulness. A total of fifteen judges are listed in the book including Deborah, Gideon, and Samson.

The entire book of Judges revolves around a pattern
that repeats itself seven times. One generation faithfully
followed the Lord but then they died. The subsequent
generations turned away from God by serving idols
which led to their oppression by another nation. When
the reality of their actions became apparent, they cried
out to God for help which He provided by sending a
judge to conquer their oppressor. After their deliverance,
they remained faithful until the judge died and a new
generation of adults emerged. At that point, the cycle
repeated itself. This pattern is summarized in Chapter 2
beginning in verse 8:

> Joshua son of Nun, the servant of the Lord,
> died at the age of a hundred and ten. And they
> buried him in the land of his inheritance, at Timnath
> Heres in the hill country of Ephraim, north of
> Mount Gaash. After that whole generation had
> been gathered to their fathers, another generation
> grew up, who knew neither the Lord nor what he
> had done for Israel. Then the Israelites did evil in
> the eyes of the Lord and served the Baals. They
> forsook the Lord, the God of their fathers, who
> had brought them out of Egypt. They followed and
> worshipped various gods of the peoples around
> them. They provoked the Lord to anger because
> they forsook him and served Baal and Ashtoreths.
> In his anger against Israel the Lord handed them
> over to raiders who plundered them.

The summary continues in verses 16-19:

> Then the Lord raised up judges who saved
> them out of the hands of these raiders. Yet they
> would not listen to their judges but prostituted

themselves to other gods and worshipped them. Unlike their fathers, they quickly turned from the way in which their fathers had walked, the way of obedience to the Lord's commands. Whenever the Lord raised up a judge for them, he was with the judge and saved them out of the hands of their enemies as long as the judge lived; for the Lord had compassion on them as they groaned under those who oppressed and afflicted them. But when the judge died, the people returned to ways even more corrupt than those of their fathers, following other gods and serving and worshipping them. They refused to give up their evil practices and stubborn ways.

Judges provides a clear illustration of what can happen when the faith that is present in one generation is not effectively passed to subsequent generations.

Ruth

In contrast to Judges, the story of Naomi and Ruth provides a wonderful illustration of the lifelong bond that can exist between individuals from different generations. The book of Ruth begins by introducing Elimelech and his wife Naomi who were living in Bethlehem with their two sons when a famine hit. In order to have enough food to survive, they decided to move to Moab where they lived for a number of years. During their stay in Moab, Naomi experienced a number of significant events. Elimelech died, her two sons were married, and then both of them died. Since her extended family was in Bethlehem and the famine had ended, Naomi decided to return to her homeland. Both of her daughters-in-law, Ruth and Orpah, wanted to go with her but after some persuasion, Orpah decided to stay in Moab. Ruth, however, insisted that she would go with Naomi and in verses 16-17 of the opening chapter she declared:

> Don't urge me to leave you or to turn back from you. Where you go I will go, and where you stay, I will stay. Your people will be my people and your God my God. Where you die I will die, and there I will be buried. May the Lord deal with me, be it ever so severely, if anything but death separates you and me.

With this strong intergenerational bond, Naomi and Ruth helped each other survive. Naomi shared her knowledge of the local culture and their extended family while Ruth used her physical abilities to gather food for both of them. During one of her trips to collect grain, Ruth was noticed by the owner of the field. When Naomi learned that the man's name was Boaz, she explained to Ruth that he could be their kinsman-redeemer and offered counsel to her during the process. Eventually, Boaz and Ruth were married and when they had a son Naomi helped to care for him.

Psalms

Multiple passages about the generations are found in the Psalms and many of them deal with passing the faith from one generation to the next. For instance, Psalm 78:1-6 says:

> O my people, hear my teaching; listen to the words of my mouth. I will open my mouth in parables, I will utter hidden things, things from of old- what we have heard and known, what our fathers told us. We will not hide them from

their children; we will tell the next generation the praiseworthy deeds of the Lord, his power, and the wonders he has done. He decreed statutes for Jacob and established the law in Israel, which he commanded our forefathers to teach their children, so the next generation would know them, even the children yet to be born, and they in turn would tell their children.

As a part of this passage, the psalmist also acknowledges that some generations are not faithful to God and their way of life should not be extended to subsequent generations (v. 7-8):

Then they would put their trust in God and would not forget his deeds but would keep his commands. They would not be like their forefathers – a stubborn and rebellious generation, whose hearts were not loyal to God, whose spirits were not faithful to him.

Other verses that echo the importance of extending the faith to subsequent generations include:

Psalm 71:18 -

Even when I am old and gray, do not forsake me O God, till I declare your power to the next generation, your might to all who are to come.

Psalm 90:1 –

Lord, you have been our dwelling place throughout all generations.

Psalm 100:5 –

For the Lord is good and his love endures forever; his faithfulness continues through all generations.

Psalm 102:18 –

Let this be written for a future generation, that a people not yet created may praise the Lord.

Psalm 145:4 –

One generation will commend your works to another; they will tell of your mighty acts.

The Gospels

During his ministry, Jesus frequently encountered resistance to his claim of being the Messiah. As a result, the Gospels are full of scathing indictments against the Jews who were more interested in defending their traditions than receiving the Son of God. The list of adjectives used to describe the generation that was rejecting him included wicked, adulterous, unbelieving, perverse, and sinful (see for instance, Matt. 12:39, Mark 8:38, and Luke 9:41).

One Jewish tradition that was particularly appalling to Jesus was the practice of Corban. According to the legal code that had emerged among the Jews, an individual could declare that his property was being dedicated to the Lord which meant that it was not available to assist older family members who were in need. The hypocrisy of this arrangement was that the property did not have to actually be offered as a sacrifice to God but could be retained for personal use.[4] Infuriated by their allegiance to tradition rather than the word of God, Jesus condemns them in Mark 7:9-12:

And he said to them: "You have a fine way of setting aside the commands of God in order to observe your own traditions! For Moses said,

'Honor your father and your mother,' and 'Anyone who curses his father or mother must be put to death.' But you say that if a man says to his father or mother: Whatever help you might otherwise have received from me is Corban (that is, a gift devoted to God), then you no longer let him do anything for his father or mother. Thus you nullify the word of God by your tradition that you have handed down. And you do many things like that."

Timothy

The life of Timothy clearly illustrates the role that older generations can have in extending the faith to younger generations. According to II Timothy 1:5, the seeds of Timothy's faith were planted and nurtured by his grandmother and mother. When the Apostle Paul came to Lystra and Derbe during his second missionary journey, the believers in that area spoke very highly of Timothy. Apparently, Paul was also very impressed with him because he wanted Timothy to join the missionary team as they continued to spread the Gospel (Acts 16:3).

Over time, Paul mentored Timothy and they developed a deep friendship that transcended their difference in age. As they traveled together, Paul's confidence in Timothy grew to the point that he left Timothy in Ephesus in order to continue teaching and leading the young church. The depth of their relationship can be seen in the opening words of I and II Timothy when Paul refers to Timothy as "… my true son in the faith" and "… my dear son." When Paul was in prison and nearing the end of his life, he longed for visitors who could offer encouragement to him and provide information about the churches he had planted but he was particularly anxious for Timothy to come to Rome. In II Timothy 4:9, he says "Do your best to come to me quickly" and in verse 21, "Do your best to get here before winter."

Titus

Titus was also a traveling companion of Paul's and during one trip he was asked to remain with the church in Crete. As Paul acknowledged in Titus 1:12, working with the Cretans was very challenging because their reputation of being "… liars, evil brutes, lazy gluttons" was well known. In this setting, Titus was supposed to help the recently planted church to mature by appointing elders and teaching sound doctrine. Paul clarified the meaning of sound doctrine beginning in Titus 2:1:

> You must teach what is in accordance with sound doctrine. Teach the older men to be temperate, worthy of self-respect, self-controlled, and sound in faith, in love and in endurance. Likewise, teach older women to be reverent in the way they live, not to be slanderers or addicted to much wine, but to teach what is good. Then they can train the younger women to love their husbands and children, to be self-controlled and pure, to be busy at home, to be kind, and to be subject to their husbands, so that no one will malign the word of God. Similarly, encourage the young men to be self-controlled.

Paul was telling Titus that the church would become healthy and strong when members of the older

generations taught members of the younger generations
how to live the Christian life based on the example they
were setting.

I Corinthians

In the twelfth chapter of I Corinthians, Paul encouraged
the Christians at Corinth to become unified even though
there was great diversity in their church. Beginning in the
twelfth verse, he used the human body as an illustration
of how the church should function:

> The body is a unit, though it is made up of
> many parts; and though all its parts are many, they
> form one body. So it is with Christ. For we were
> all baptized by one Spirit into one body – whether
> Jews or Greeks, slave or free – and we were all
> given the one Spirit to drink. Now the body is
> not made up of one part but of many. If the foot
> should say, "Because I am not a hand, I do not
> belong to the body," it would not for that reason
> cease to be part of the body. And if the ear should
> say, "Because I am not an eye, I do not belong to
> the body," it would not for that reason cease to
> be part of the body. If the whole body were an
> eye, where would the sense of hearing be? If the
> whole body were an ear, where would the sense of
> smell be? But in fact God has arranged the parts
> in the body, every one of them, just as he wanted
> them to be.

Typically, this passage is applied to individuals and
the use of their gifts in the church. However, it is also
applicable to generations because some churches have as
many as five different generations trying to function as

one body. As was seen in the previous chapters, each generation brings a unique perspective to the church based on their shared life experiences which results in great diversity of thought. Many churches struggle with the task of understanding the generations and bringing them together into a community of faith like Paul was describing. Nevertheless, I Corinthians 12 describes the Biblical model and it is the one that every congregation should strive to emulate.

Summary

Our culture tries to convince us that a generation gap exists which cannot be bridged. In contrast, the Bible clearly communicates that the church has been designed to bring the generations together. Developing an intergenerational community of faith can be challenging but as we will see in Chapter 9, it is certainly attainable.

Chapter 9
A Congregational Response

Having been introduced to the forces that shaped the five living generations and with an understanding of what the Bible says about the topic, it is now possible to apply the information to the local church. An initial step that a congregation should take is to determine how "generation-friendly" it is. In order to do this, it is helpful to think of a continuum.[1] At one end of the continuum is the *inherited* church that relies heavily on the past to guide its future. Programs and practices that have been in place for many years continue to be used and the prevailing mindset is that if something worked in the past it will certainly work in the future. While an inherited church usually consists of a large number of individuals from the pre-World War II generations, it often has members from the other generations, as well. The presence of multiple generations may lead the members of an inherited church to conclude that they are a blended church. In reality, they are not because the primary focus of their church is to maintain the methods they have used in the past. Individuals from any generation are welcome to be a part of an inherited church but they must share the conviction that traditional methods of evangelism and worship are still the most appropriate to use.

A simple illustration of this approach is the gospel meeting. For years, one of the most effective ways to reach the unchurched was to hold a gospel meeting. A visiting evangelist would come to town and preach for several consecutive nights. Members of the local church would canvass the community with advertisements and personal invitations to attend the meeting. Since the range of alternate activities was fairly limited, attendance at the meeting was usually high as was the number of conversions. However, as the number of dual-income families began to grow and the scope of after-school activities for children expanded, fewer individuals were able to attend a multi-night gospel meeting. For those who witnessed the effectiveness of the gospel meeting, the decision to evangelize a community using other methods has been met with great resistance. In their eyes, gospel meetings worked in the past and they will continue to work if the right speaker is brought in and enough effort is put forth by the members. While this level of persistence is admirable, it fails to consider that other methods of communicating the good news of Jesus exist which are more relevant to contemporary culture.

Generation-Specific

At the other end of the continuum is the *generation-specific* church. In contrast to the emphasis on tradition that is seen in an inherited church, most generation-specific churches are driven by a desire to be culturally-relevant in their practices and programs. Traditional forms of music and worship are rarely seen in the generation-specific church. The use of hymnals, deeply theological sermons, and official-sounding titles are replaced with praise songs, life application lessons, and ministers who are referred to by their first name. The majority of generation-specific churches are targeted to Baby Boomers or GenXers and they often have a non-denominational name attached to them. Descriptors like "community church", "fellowship church", or "Bible church" are seen quite commonly as the generation-specific church tries to communicate the fresh approach they are taking to religion.

It is important to note that while many generation-specific churches have made a conscious choice to target one group, some churches become generation-specific due to demographic realities. In numerous communities, churches that were once active and growing have seen their membership decline and age in place. A primary reason for this is because the population in that area has done the same thing. Younger individuals and families have moved in search of greater job opportunities and the community is left with a diminishing population. The church is not the only social institution to experience this as school consolidation has been taking place for years in rural areas as the population continues to shift to suburban and urban locations. When a church becomes generation-specific due to demographic factors, there are very few options available for countering the decline. Efforts to minister with the members of the community should certainly continue but unless a significant population reversal occurs, the future of the church in that location is very uncertain.

For churches that choose to be generation-specific, their future is also perilous but for a different reason. The concept of a generation-specific church is inherently flawed because the generation that was originally targeted will continue to move through the life cycle and their needs will change. For instance, a church that was formed in order to appeal to GenXers when they were young professionals either disbanded or expanded its mission when they started families. The initial focus of the church was on young, single individuals with little consideration for children. Thus, the scheduled fellowships, length and content of the worship service, and scope of ancillary programs all centered around the lifestyle of persons in their late teens and early to mid 20s. With the arrival of children, GenXers had to rearrange their priorities and a new set of criteria influenced where they worshipped. Attended nurseries, cradle roll classes, and pre-school programs became far more important to them and the generation-specific church either adapted to these new expectations or watched its members leave.

Blended

Between the two extremes is the *blended* church. As its name suggests, the blended church seeks to bring together the two extremes and create an environment in which all of the generations are appreciated. In order to accomplish this, the views of each generation must be taken into consideration when planning the worship assembly and determining the range of programs to be offered by a church. Based on the information presented in Chapter 8, the blended church is the most biblical option on the continuum. In line with Paul's instruction in I Corinthians 12, each generation in the blended church is valued and as the parts learn to function together, the body becomes stronger.

While recognizing the desirability of the blended church, it is important to acknowledge the challenges that must be overcome in order to achieve it. Since as many as five generational perspectives are present, a blended church will often have a fragile existence as inherited views and contemporary culture interface. Every activity in which the church engages has the potential of becoming a battleground depending on the dynamics that were in place before the process of blending began.[2] In order to avoid the conflicts, some churches try to accommodate the generations without really blending them. A prime example of this approach is when two worship assemblies are offered even though the auditorium is large enough to seat all of the members and visitors at one time. A traditional worship service is available for those who desire to sing hymns, hear a sermon, and dress in more formal clothes. The contemporary service usually follows and is attended by individuals who wear more casual clothes, sing praise songs, and hear a life application lesson. A careful examination of those in attendance reveals that the traditional service is usually favored by members of the pre-World War II generations and the contemporary service is the choice of Boomers, GenXers, and Millennials. In other words, while it appears that a blended church exists in reality there are two fellowships that happen to share the same building.[3]

The Issue of Change

On the way to becoming a blended church, many congregations encounter the challenges that are inevitable when five different generations bring their perspectives into one setting. However, for a church to truly be blended each of the five perspectives must be woven into the fabric of the congregation and one perspective cannot dominate the others. When the reality of this arrangement sets in, tensions often increase and conflict may ensue particularly when changes are proposed for the worship service. To illustrate this point, consider the information I obtained during a recent survey of more than one thousand Protestant church members from across the country. When asked to indicate the style of music they preferred in a church service, 67% of the Senior Adults and 67% of the Builders indicated that they preferred traditional music which was defined as singing from a hymnal. Only 42% of Boomers and 33% of GenXers favored traditional music opting instead for contemporary music like praise songs. Information on the Millennials was not available since the study focused on adults and the vast majority of Millennials had not reached the age of 18 when the data collection occurred.

A similar pattern was seen when the style of worship was considered as 67% of Senior Adults and 66% of Builders indicated a preference for a traditional service which was defined as using a hymnal, hearing a sermon, and having a more formal atmosphere. In contrast, only 49% of Boomers and 40% of GenXers favored a traditional worship setting opting instead for a more participatory and visually-oriented service.

This information illustrates how the generational perspectives can manifest themselves in the local church. It also serves as a reminder that achieving a blended church can be very challenging. Strong leadership and a commitment to prayer are needed in order to handle the conflicts that are likely to appear. Church leaders will need to be patient and exercise a tremendous degree of wisdom as they guide the process of change that will be very disconcerting to some. At the individual level, each of the members will need to make an honest assessment of their views and determine the degree to which they are based on preferences rather than Biblical mandates.

Becoming Blended

Becoming a blended church can be difficult especially when all five generations are involved. However, blended churches are in a much better position to sustain long-term growth because they appeal to a wider audience and have developed the ability to navigate the winds of change.[4] As a church becomes blended, an intergenerational culture will begin to emerge. In order to encourage this development, a church should implement the following recommendations.

Understand the Perspectives

This book began by discussing how generational perspectives develop and why they are so powerful. In Chapters 3 through 7, the forces that shaped the five living generations were presented along with a discussion of the key components of each generational lens. Church leaders and members should become thoroughly acquainted with these perspectives beginning with their own. As they do, the generation gap will begin to close because the level of understanding among members of the various generations will increase exponentially. For those who would like to develop a deeper understanding of the generations and their impact on the church, the work of several outstanding authors is identified in Appendix A.

Appreciate God's Plan

Our God expects His church to consist of multiple generations and to be characterized by positive intergenerational contact. This message is presented repeatedly in the Old and New Testaments and remains applicable today. When Moses spoke to the Israelites for the final time, he emphasized the importance of the older generations transmitting their faith to the younger generations and Judges shows what can happen when one generation does not effectively communicate with subsequent generations. In the New Testament, the Apostle Paul not only instructed churches to develop positive intergenerational relationships, he created them with Titus and Timothy.

The modern church has a golden opportunity to implement these teachings since the dynamics of family life in America have changed. Many nuclear families are stretched to their limit as both dad and mom are working full-time and trying to be actively involved in the life of their children. While extended family members are often willing to help, the geographic distance that separates many of them prohibits active involvement in the daily life of their children and grandchildren. The church can fill this void by creating strong, intergenerational fellowships in which the members feel comfortable sharing the joys and burdens of life.

Encourage Intergenerational Contact

Many of the negative stereotypes that are used to describe a generation stem from indirect information. For instance, Senior Adults may draw conclusions about Millennials (and vice versa) based on what they have read, heard, or casually observed. Noticeably absent from their evaluation is information that has come from their direct interaction with members of that generation. A church can help to remedy this situation by providing opportunities for positive, intergenerational contact. One way to do this is to have individuals from multiple generations lead the worship service. Many churches do this by default but never really draw attention to it. From time to time, an intergenerational worship service should be planned and special attention focused on the breadth of generations in that church. Some congregations find that National Grandparents Day, which is the first Sunday after Labor Day, is an opportune time to do this. The theme for the day is God's faithfulness to all the generations which helps to raise awareness of the common ground that is shared by individuals who believe in the risen Christ.

Churches can also schedule intergenerational events which include activities that occur annually or bi-annually. The range of possibilities is endless and may include a "sweetheart banquet" where Senior Adults or Builders are served a meal and entertained by GenXers or Millennials. Intergenerational service projects provide an opportunity for individuals from different generations to work side by side and communicate with one another. A few churches have even developed intergenerational retreats in which the generations participate in activities that enhance their spiritual and social relationships.

While intergenerational *events* occur once or twice a year, intergenerational *programs* are more continuous in nature. A popular option under this heading is "adopt a grandparent" or "adopt a grandchild" efforts which are meant to create a link between members of different generations. In a typical arrangement, a young Millennial is paired with a Builder or Senior Adult. While the initial commitment is for one year, it is not uncommon for the relationships to continue for many years because of the mutually beneficial exchanges that take place.

A second type of intergenerational program is the creation of teaching teams in which individuals from different generations work together in a classroom setting. One member of the team can be designated as the teacher and the other as the assistant or the two can co-teach a class by alternating weeks, months, or quarters. Depending on the age of the students, the intergenerational teaching team might bring as many as three generations together in one setting. This approach can also be adapted to adult Bible classes particularly when life stage issues are being studied. For instance, a class focused on God's plan for parenting would be most effective when those who were raising children were able to exchange ideas with individuals whose children were grown.

Another intergenerational program option is to have Millennials or GenXers conduct life story interviews with Builders or Senior Adults. The interviews could be summarized in written form and assembled in a book that other members of the congregation could read. This activity would connect multiple generations and allow the history of the individuals, as well as the church, to be passed down to future generations. A program like this is ideal for the summer months when school is out and young people have more time to dedicate to the project.

Monitor the Numbers

A church should also monitor the demographic composition of its members and the community in which it is located. Chapters 3 through 7 described the five living generations and the percentage of the American population that falls into each group. As a reminder:

*Senior Adults – 5%

*Builders – 14%

*Boomers – 27%
*GenXers – 27%
*Millennials – 27%

Very few churches will perfectly mirror these figures but they provide guidelines for having a balanced representation of the generations in a congregation.

If the birth year of the members is known, then a total number for each generation can be determined. Next, the number for each generation can be divided by the total number for the church in order to determine the percentage of the membership that falls into each generation. For instance, if there are 75 Builders in a church with a total membership of 300, then they would represent 25% of the congregation. By doing this, a church will know how well their membership is distributed across the generations and steps can be taken to reach out to a generation that is underrepresented.

Monitoring the demographic composition of the surrounding community can also be done by using information from the United States Census Bureau. The steps involved in doing this are:

*Go to the internet and type *www.census.gov*
*Select "American Fact Finder" from the opening page
*Search by "Street Address"
*Choose "Census 2000"
*Type a street address
*Choose a "Geography"

Various levels of information are available but the "county", "county subdivision", or "census tract" options will be the most appropriate to use. To see the area that

is covered by the level of analysis that has been selected, click on "Reference Maps." Then, go to the "Quick Tables & Demographic Profiles" section and choose one of the following:
*DP-1 (Profile of General Demographic Characteristics: 2000)
*DP-2 (Profile of Selected Social Characteristics: 2000)
*DP-3 (Profile of Selected Economic Characteristics: 2000)

While a number of other tables exist, these will provide extremely valuable information about the residents who live in the surrounding neighborhoods. The presence of the various generations can be determined by looking at the ages shown in DP-1. Since this data is from the 2000 Census, the range of ages in each generation will be:
*Senior Adults = 74 or higher
*Builders = 55-73
*Boomers = 36-54
*GenXers = 17-35
*Millennials = 1-16
One or two years of some generations will be lost since the Census Bureau grouped the ages but this exercise will provide a revealing look at the community in which a church is located.

Engage and Evangelize

Many Senior Adults and Builders have displayed an amazing level of loyalty to their respective congregations through attendance, contributions, and service but a process of disengagement from active involvement often occurs as they get older. When this happens, the wisdom of the Senior Adults and Builders is lost and an important link in building an intergenerational church is broken. As a result, congregations must be committed to ministry *with* their older members not just *to* them so that they remain fully engaged in the life and work of the church.

As noted in Chapter 5, some Boomers have remained loyal to a church throughout their life but many are returning after a long absence. As a church attempts to reach out to Boomers, they should bear in mind that Boomers want to be involved in programs and activities that are organized, high in quality, and connected to their local community. They are attracted to a church that can clearly articulate its purpose and how its ministries are designed to fulfill that purpose. Boomers are also attracted to a church where they can develop ministries based on their life experiences so Bible classes and weekend seminars organized around issues such as raising teenagers, single parenting, divorce recovery, blended families, and caregiving are particularly appealing.

Since many GenXers were not raised in church-going families, evangelism is an important consideration followed very closely by engagement. Friendship evangelism resonates with GenXers as does narrative evangelism which involves an individual telling their personal story of conversion. Once GenXers are introduced to the Gospel and become involved in a church, building authentic relationships is the key to their further engagement. GenXers will bring a healthy dose of skepticism with them so it is up to the members of the church to convince them that their faith is genuine and their interest in others is sincere. An effective way to do this is by creating small group settings where GenXers can develop meaningful friendships with their peers as well as individuals from other generations.

As Millennials mature, the most effective way to engage them in the life of an intergenerational church will become more apparent. At this point, their commitment to diversity and teamwork should be incorporated into the activities of the church. In addition, the highly visual and technologically-sophisticated world in which they live should be acknowledged by church leaders and appropriate adjustments made to the manner in which the worship assembly is conducted.

Summary

Despite what some individuals may suggest, a simple formula for blending the generations in a church does not exist. The history, size, leadership style, and informal power bases of a church will impact the speed with which the process can be undertaken and the most appropriate methods to be used.[5] Nevertheless, a congregation that desires to blend the generations should follow the recommendations given in this chapter while maintaining an awareness of the idiosyncrasies of their situation. Each church will need to determine the right mix of intergenerational activities and recognize that the ultimate success of their efforts will be the result of God's blessing.

Epilogue

For those who are interested in gaining a more in-depth understanding of the generations, a number of excellent books are identified in Appendix A. Since the labels used to describe each generation will vary from one source to another, a synopsis of synonyms and sub-groups is provided below.

Many authors do not distinguish between Senior Adults and Builders opting instead to create one category for individuals born prior to 1946. The main label of Builders or Pre-Boomers is then divided into the G. I. Generation (pre-1925), Silent Generation (1926-1939), and War Babies (1940-1945).[1]

Individuals born between 1946 and 1964 are most commonly referred to as Baby Boomers. Within the span of the generation, a distinction is often made between Leading Edge Boomers (1946-1954) and Trailing Edge Boomers (1955-1964).[2]

When Douglas Coupland's novel, *Generation X*, was published in 1991, the book's title became a popular label for those born between 1965 and 1983.[3] Another popular name has been Baby Busters since the number of babies born during this span was noticeably lower than during the Baby Boom years. A number of other names have also been used including 13ers (the 13th generation since the founding of America) and the Echo Boom (a spike in births occurred when Trailing Edge Boomers began having children). The generation is often divided into the Bust (1965-1976) and the Baby Boomlet (1977-1983).[4]

The name Millennials is generally attributed to Howe and Strauss but a litany of synonyms exists for those born between 1984 and 2002.[5] George Barna prefers Mosaics since this generation is the most racially and ethnically diverse in the history of the United States.[6] Thom Rainer labels them as the Bridger Generation since they bridge the 20th and 21st centuries, as well as the second and third millennium.[7] Other names include Generation Y (followed Generation X), NetGen (were raised on the Internet), and Generation E (business leaders see them as future entrepreneurs). Rather than using one label for the entire generation, some authors use the name Generation Y for those born from 1984 to 1993 and Millennials for those born between 1994 and 2002.[8]

Since the last Millennial was born in 2002, a sixth generation has begun. Known as Generation Z,[9] they are the children of the youngest GenXers and the oldest Millennials. At this point, it is impossible to identify the characteristics of Generation Z since they are so young but some intriguing observations can be made about their entrance into the world. Generation Z is the first to be born and raised entirely in the 21st century. As a result, events such as the Civil Rights Movement, the fall of the Berlin Wall, and the indiscretions of President Clinton will be historical information for them. Even more stunning, though, is that the events of September 11, 2001 also occurred prior to their arrival.

Second, Generation Z will be members of the most diverse population in American history. Pluralism has replaced assimilation as the philosophy that is applied to immigrants. Rather than requiring the newly arrived to become like the dominant group, Americans are more willing to allow multiple languages and belief systems to exist simultaneously with the mainstream culture.

Third, members of Generation Z will be part of the oldest population in the history of the United States. On one hand, if the aging of the Senior Adult and Builder generations is straining government programs and services, one can only imagine the impact that Baby Boomers will have in their seventh, eighth, and ninth decades of life. On the other hand, Generation Z will be able to enjoy the rich tapestry that accompanies a society in which the older members connect the younger members with their national, religious, and personal heritage.

Finally, Generation Z will be the most technologically sophisticated group the world has ever seen. While GenXers were exposed to computers in high school and Millennials learned to use them in grade school, the majority of Generation Z will be computer literate by their first day of kindergarten. The benefits of this level of knowledge are enormous but they do not come free of charge. One of the great unknowns about Generation Z is whether their ability to interact in face-to-face settings will be adversely affected by the technological advancements.

Appendix A
Resources

Barna, G. (2001). *Real Teens: A Contemporary Snapshot of Youth Culture*. Ventura, CA: Regal Books.

Barna, G. (1994). *Baby Busters: The Disillusioned Generation*. Chicago, IL: Northfield Publishing.

Carroll, J. W., & Roof, W. C. (2002). *Bridging Divided Worlds: Generational Cultures in Congregations*. San Francisco: Jossey-Bass.

Coupland, D. (1991). *Generation X: Tales for an Accelerated Culture*. New York: St. Martin's Press.

Dychtwald, K. (1999). *Age Power: How the 21st Century Will Be Ruled by the New Old*. New York, NY: Jeremy P. Tarcher/Putnam.

Flory, R., & Miller, D. (2000). *Gen X Religion*. New York: Rutledge.

Grenz, S. J. (1996). *A Primer on Postmodernism*. Grand Rapids, MI: William B. Eerdmans Publishing Company.

Howe, N., & Strauss, W. (2000). *Millennials Rising: The Next Great Generation*. New York: Vintage Books.

Kallen, S., A. (2002). *The Baby Boom.* San Diego, CA: Greenhaven Press.

Knapp, J. L. (2003). *The Graying of the Flock: A New Model for Ministry.* Orange, CA: Leafwood Press.

McIntosh, G. L. (2002). *One Church: Four Generations.* Grand Rapids, MI: Baker House Books.

Mead, M. (1970). *Culture and Commitment: A Study of the Generation Gap.* Garden City, NY: Natural History Press/Doubleday & Company, Inc.

Rainer, T. S. (1997). *The Bridger Generation: America's Second Largest Generation, What They Believe, How to Reach Them.* Nashville, TN: Broadman & Holman Publishers.

Roof, W. C. (1999). *Spiritual Marketplace: Baby Boomers and the Remaking of American Religion.* Princeton, NJ: Princeton University Press.

Roof, W. C. (1993). *A Generation of Seekers: The Spiritual Journeys of the Baby Boom Generation.* San Francisco, CA: Harper Collins Publishers.

Smith, J. W., & Clurman, A. (1997). *Rocking the Ages: The Yankelovich Report on Generational Marketing.* New York: Harper Business.

Whitesel, B., & Hunter, K. R. (2000). *A House Divided: Bridging the Generation Gaps in Your Church.* Nashville, TN: Abingdon Press.

Wuthnow, R. (1998). *After Heaven: Spirituality in America Since the 1950s.* Berkeley, CA: University of California Press.

Wuthnow, R. (1988). *The Restructuring of American Religion.* Princeton, NJ: Princeton University Press.

Appendix B
Methodology

The data used in the analysis were gathered using a multistage sampling technique. During the summer of 2002, nationally representative sampling frames were identified for Church of Christ, Presbyterian, Southern Baptist, and United Methodist congregations and a random sample of one hundred churches was drawn from each fellowship. The main criterion for inclusion in the sample was a membership of at least 350. A letter was sent to each of the churches explaining the purpose of the research and asking for permission to survey the adult members of their congregation. From the list of churches that responded in the affirmative, a sample of eighteen congregations was drawn guided primarily by the desire to have a balanced number of respondents from each fellowship as well as geographical diversity.

A contact person was identified at each church who served as the liaison between the members and the author. Based on the liaison's estimate, a box containing surveys and envelopes was sent to the church office and distributed to the members. Though the method of distributing and retrieving the surveys varied from site to site, every effort was made to ensure that every adult member was given the opportunity to participate in the study. In order to ensure confidentiality, each participant was asked to complete the survey, seal it in the envelope that was provided, and return it to a central location designated by the liaison. Following a two week data collection period, the liaison mailed all of the completed surveys to the author who tabulated the results and analyzed the responses using SPSS (Statistical Package for the Social Sciences).

The survey consisted of a variety of questions dealing with social and religious issues, as well as demographic information. Provided below is a summary of key demographic information:

Total Respondents	1,089
Senior Adults	153
Builders	447
Boomers	351
GenXers	97

Fellowship

Church of Christ	295
Presbyterian	241
Southern Baptist	192
United Methodist	361

Gender

Male	433
Female	636

Age

Mean	58.09
Standard Deviation	16.01

Chapter Notes

Chapter 1

[1] Mead, M. (1970). *Culture and Commitment: A Study of the Generation Gap.* Garden City, NY: Natural History Press/Doubleday & Company, Inc. p. 1.

[2] ibid, pp. 2 and 63.

[3] Carroll, J. W., & Roof, W. C. (2002). *Bridging Divided Worlds: Generational Cultures in Congregations.* San Francisco: Jossey-Bass, p. 6.

[4] Smith, J. W., & Clurman, A. (1997). *Rocking the Ages: The Yankelovich Report on Generational Marketing.* New York: Harper Business, p. 8.

[5] Since the Millennial generation ended in 2002, it can be argued that a sixth generation has begun.
United States Census Bureau (2003). *Statistical Abstracts of the United States: 2003.* Washington, DC, Table #14.

[6] Miller, D. E., & Miller, A. M. (2000). Understanding Generation X: Values, Politics, and Religious Commitments. In R. Flory and D. Miller (eds.), *Gen X Religion*, New York: Rutledge, p. 6.

Chapter 2

[1] Caplow, T., Hicks, L., & Wattenberg, B. J. (2001). *The First Measured Century.* Washington, DC: American

Enterprise Institute, pp. 164-165.

[2] ibid, pp. 26-27.

[3] ibid, pp. 26-27.

[4] ibid, pp. 12-13.

[5] ibid, pp. 84-85.

[6] Macionis, J. J. (2002). *Society: The Basics* (6th ed.). Upper Saddle River, NJ: Pearson Education, p. 166.

[7] Caplow, T., Hicks, L., & Wattenberg, B. J. (2001). *The First Measured Century*. Washington, DC: American Enterprise Institute, pp. 38-39.

[8] ibid, pp. 80-81.

[9] ibid, p. 72.

[10] Myers, D. G. (2000). *The American Paradox: Spiritual Hunger in an Age of Plenty*. New Haven, CT: Yale Nota Bene, p.68.

[11] Caplow, T., Hicks, L., & Wattenberg, B. J. (2001). *The First Measured Century*. Washington, DC: American Enterprise Institute, pp. 52-53.

[12] ibid, pp. 52-53.

[13] ibid, p. 99.

[14] ibid, p. 99.

[15] ibid, p. 99.

[16] ibid, p. 100.

[17] ibid, pp. 276-277.

[18] Wuthnow, R. (1988). *The Restructuring of American Religion*. Princeton, NJ: Princeton University Press, pp. 21-26.

[19] ibid, pp. 15-16.

[20] Wuthnow, R. (1988). *The Restructuring of American Religion*. Princeton, NJ: Princeton University Press, pp. 18-19.

[21] Wuthnow, R. (1998). *After Heaven: Spirituality in America Since the 1950s*. Berkeley, CA: University of California Press, p. 39.

[22] Roof, W. C. (1999). *Spiritual Marketplace: Baby Boomers and the Remaking of American Religion.* Princeton, NJ: Princeton University Press, pp. 9-10.

[23] Grenz, S. J. (1996). *A Primer on Postmodernism.* Grand Rapids, MI: William B. Eerdmans Publishing Company, pp. 58-60.

[24] Ritzer, G. (1992). *Sociological Theory* (3rd ed.). New York, NY: McGraw-Hill, p. 11.

[25] Grenz, S. J. (1996). *A Primer on Postmodernism.* Grand Rapids, MI: William B. Eerdmans Publishing Company, p. 81.

[26] See for instance:

Rose, M. (1992). Defining the Post-Modern. In C. Jencks (Ed.), *The Post-Modern Reader,* pp. 119-136. New York, NY: St. Martin's Press.

Jencks, C. (1989). *What is Post-Modernism* (3rd ed.). New York, NY: St. Martin's Press.

[27] Grenz, S. J. (1996). *A Primer on Postmodernism.* Grand Rapids, MI: William B. Eerdmans Publishing Company, p. 12.

[28] ibid, pp. 7-8.

[29] ibid, p. 14.

Chapter 3

[1] Gross, D. (1996). *Forbes Greatest Business Stories of All Time.* Hoboken, NJ: John Wiley & Sons, pp. 74-89.

[2] Anthony Center For Women's Leadership (2004). *U.S. Suffrage Movement Timeline,* University of Rochester (New York): www.rochester.edu/SBA/timeline1.html.

[3] Smith, P. (2000). Prohibition Dries Up a Thirsty Nation. In J. Wukovits (ed.), *The 1920s,* San Diego, CA: Greenhaven Press, pp. 111-117.

[4] ibid, p. 116.

[5] United States Bureau of the Census (1920). Volumes I & II. Washington, DC: Government Printing Office.

Chapter 4

[1] Watkins, T. H. (2000). Depression Farming: Drought, Dust, and Displacement. In L. Gerdes (ed.), *The 1930s*, San Diego, CA: Greenhaven Press, pp. 90-96.

[2] ibid, pp. 97-98.

[3] Brinkley, A. (2000). A New Deal for the American People. In L. Gerdes (ed.), *The 1930s*, San Diego, CA: Greenhaven Press, pp. 110-118.

Jackson, D. D. (2000). Life in the Civilian Conservation Corps. In L. Gerdes (ed.), *The 1930s*, San Diego, CA: Greenhaven Press, pp. 132-143.

[4] Phillips, C. (2000). December 7, 1941: A Day of Infamy. In L. Gerdes (ed.), *The 1940s*, San Diego, CA: Greenhaven Press, pp. 62-79.

[5] Lingeman, R. R. (2000). Shortages, Conservatism, and Rationing. In L. Gerdes (ed.), *The 1940s*, San Diego, CA: Greenhaven Press, pp. 163-176.

[6] United States Bureau of the Census (1940). Volume II (Part I). Washington, DC: Government Printing Office.

United States Bureau of the Census (1943). Statistical Abstracts of the United States – 1943. Washington, DC: Government Printing Office.

Chapter 5

[1] www.now.org/history/history.html

[2] Miller, D. T., & Nowak, M. (2002). A New Kind of Music. In S. A Kallen (ed.), *The Baby Boom*, San Diego, CA: Greenhaven Press, pp. 51-52.

[3] Halberstam, D. (1993). *The Fifties*. New York, NY: Villard, p. 471.

[4] Kallen, S. A. (2002). Introduction: The Influences of a Generation. In S. A Kallen (ed.), *The Baby Boom*, San Diego, CA: Greenhaven Press, p. 17.

[5] Dychtwald, K. (1999). *Age Power: How the 21st Century Will Be Ruled by the New Old*. New York, NY: Jeremy P. Tarcher/Putnam, p. 63.

[6] Miller, D. T., & Nowak, M. (2002). A New Kind of Music. In S. A Kallen (ed.), *The Baby Boom*, San Diego, CA: Greenhaven Press, p. 50.

[7] Roof, W. C. (1992). The Baby Boom's Search for God. *American Demographics*, 14(12), pp. 1-6.

[8] United States Bureau of the Census (1976). Historical Statistics of the United States: Colonial Times to 1970 (Part I). Washington, DC: Government Printing Office.

[9] United States Bureau of the Census (1960). Volume I – Characteristics of the Population. Washington, DC: Government Printing Office.

[10] Roof, W. C. (1993). *A Generation of Seekers: The Spiritual Journeys of the Baby Boom Generation*. San Francisco, CA: Harper Collins Publishers.

Roof, W. C. (1999). *Spiritual Marketplace: Baby Boomers and the Remaking of American Religion*. Princeton, NJ: Princeton University Press.

Chapter 6

[1] Thurber, K. T., Jr. (2000). The Personal Computer Revolution. In J. Torr (ed.), *The 1980s*, San Diego, CA: Greenhaven Press, pp. 150-156.

[2] Marty, M. A. (2000). Pop Culture in the 80s: Plenty of Pleasant Distractions. In J. Torr (ed.), *The 1980s*, San Diego, CA: Greenhaven Press, pp. 179-180.

Friedlander, P. (2000). The Revolution Will be Televised: Pop Music of the 80s. In J. Torr (ed.), *The 1980s*, San Diego, CA: Greenhaven Press, p. 191. http://iml.jou.ufl.edu/projects/Fall98/Hatcher/

[3] Stirn, A. (2003). Body piercing: Medical consequences and psychological motivations. *The Lancet, 361*, p. 1207.

[4] Greif, J., Hewitt, W., & Armstrong, M. L. (1999). Tattooing and body piercing: Body art practices among college students. *Clinical Nursing Research, 8*(4), p. 368.

[5] ibid, p. 369.

[6] United States Bureau of the Census (1983). General Social and Economic Characteristics. Washington, DC: Government Printing Office.

[7] Miller, D. E., & Miller, A. M. (2000). Understanding Generation X: Values, Politics, and Religious Commitments. In R. Flory & D. Miller (eds.), *GenX Religion*, New York: Routledge, p. 6.

[8] ibid, p. 4.

[9] ibid, p. 4.

[10] Carroll, J. W., & Roof, W. C. (2002). *Bridging Divided Worlds: Generational Cultures in Congregations.* San Francisco: Jossey-Bass, p. 26.

Miller, D. E., & Miller, A. M. (2000). Understanding Generation X: Values, Politics, and Religious Commitments. In R. Flory & D. Miller (eds.), *GenX Religion*, New York: Routledge, p. 5.

Barna, G. (1994). *Baby Busters: The Disillusioned Generation.* Chicago, IL: Northfield Publishing, p. 52.

[11] Whitesel, B., & Hunter, K. R. (2000). *A House Divided: Bridging the Generation Gaps in Your Church.* Nashville, TN: Abingdon Press, p. 62.

Miller, D. E., & Miller, A. M. (2000). Understanding Generation X: Values, Politics, and Religious Commitments. In R. Flory & D. Miller (eds.), *GenX Religion*, New York: Routledge, p. 10.

[12] Carroll, J. W., & Roof, W. C. (2002). *Bridging Divided Worlds: Generational Cultures in Congregations.* San Francisco: Jossey-Bass, p. 101.

Chapter 7

[1] www.ed.gov/pubs/NatAtRisk/risk.html

[2] www.cnn.com/SPECIALS/1998/schools/

[3] www.cnn.com/US/9806/12/school.shooting.verdict/
www.cnn.com/US/9712/02/school.shooting.on/

[4] www.cnn.com/US/9803/24/school.shooting

[5] www.cnn.com/SPECIALS/1998/schools/

[6] www.september11victims.com/september11victims/

[7] http://www.census.gov/hhes/income/earnings/Call1usboth.html

[8] Barna, G. (2001). *Real Teens: A Contemporary Snapshot of Youth Culture.* Ventura, CA: Regal Books, p. 43.
McIntosh, G. L. (2002). *One Church: Four Generations.* Grand Rapids, MI: Baker House Books, p. 173.

[9] Howe, N., & Strauss, W. (2000). *Millennials Rising: The Next Great Generation.* New York: Vintage Books, p. 4.

[10] Barna, G. (2001). *Real Teens: A Contemporary Snapshot of Youth Culture.* Ventura, CA: Regal Books, p. 23.
Howe, N., & Strauss, W. (2000). *Millennials Rising: The Next Great Generation.* New York: Vintage Books, p. 4.

[11] McIntosh, G. L. (2002). *One Church: Four Generations.* Grand Rapids, MI: Baker House Books, p. 172.
Howe, N., & Strauss, W. (2000). *Millennials Rising: The Next Great Generation.* New York: Vintage Books, p. 15.

[12] Howe, N., & Strauss, W. (2000). *Millennials Rising: The Next Great Generation.* New York: Vintage Books, p. 216.

[13] Barna, G. (2001). *Real Teens: A Contemporary Snapshot of Youth Culture.* Ventura, CA: Regal Books, p. 137.

Chapter 8

[1] Bromiley, G. W. (1982). *The International Standard Bible Encyclopedia* (Vol. 2). Grand Rapids, MI: William B. Eerdmans Publishing Company, p. 431.

[2] ibid, p. 431;
Achtemeier, P. J. (1985). *Harper's Bible Dictionary.* San Francisco, CA: Harper & Row, pp. 335-336.

[3] Strong, J. (1955). *The Exhaustive Concordance of the Bible.* New York: Abingdon Press, pp. 382-383.

[4] Bromiley, G. W. (1982). *The International Standard Bible Encyclopedia* (Vol. 2). Grand Rapids, MI: William B. Eerdmans Publishing Company, p. 772.

Chapter 9

[1] The continuum is drawn from:
Carroll, J. W., & Roof, W. C. (2002). *Bridging Divided Worlds: Generational Cultures in Congregations.* San Francisco: Jossey-Bass, pp. 12-13 and 105-106.
A similar concept is introduced in:
McIntosh, G. L. (2002). *One Church: Four Generations.* Grand Rapids, MI: Baker House Books, pp. 211-222.
Whitesel, B., & Hunter, K. R. (2000). *A House Divided: Bridging the Generation Gaps in Your Church.* Nashville, TN: Abingdon Press, pp. 40-55.

² Carroll, J. W., & Roof, W. C. (2002). *Bridging Divided Worlds: Generational Cultures in Congregations.* San Francisco: Jossey-Bass, p. 10.

³ Whitesel & Hunter advocate parallel worship services for the generations rather than blending (p. 222).

⁴ Carroll, J. W., & Roof, W. C. (2002). *Bridging Divided Worlds: Generational Cultures in Congregations.* San Francisco: Jossey-Bass, p. 170.

⁵ ibid, p. 212.

Epilogue

¹ McIntosh, G. L. (2002). *One Church: Four Generations.* Grand Rapids, MI: Baker House Books.

Carroll, J. W., & Roof, W. C. (2002). *Bridging Divided Worlds: Generational Cultures in Congregations.* San Francisco: Jossey-Bass.

² McIntosh, G. L. (2002). *One Church: Four Generations.* Grand Rapids, MI: Baker House Books.

³ Coupland, D. (1991). *Generation X: Tales for an Accelerated Culture.* New York: St. Martin's Press.

⁴ McIntosh, G. L. (2002). *One Church: Four Generations.* Grand Rapids, MI: Baker House Books.

⁵ Howe, N., & Strauss, W. (2000). *Millennials Rising: The Next Great Generation.* New York: Vintage Books.

⁶ Barna, G. (2001). *Real Teens: A Contemporary Snapshot of Youth Culture.* Ventura, CA: Regal Books.

⁷ Rainer, T. S. (1997). *The Bridger Generation: America's Second Largest Generation, What They Believe, How to Reach Them.* Nashville, TN: Broadman & Holman Publishers.

⁸ McIntosh, G. L. (2002). *One Church: Four Generations.* Grand Rapids, MI: Baker House Books.

⁹ Wellner, A. S. (2000). Generation Z. *American Demographics*, 22(9), p. 60.

LaVergne, TN USA
17 February 2010
173388LV00003B/23/A